2 to 22 DAYS IN GREAT BRITAIN

THE ITINERARY PLANNER
1994 Edition

RICK STEVES

John Muir Publications
Santa Fe, New Mexico

W9-AXY-347

Originally published as *22 Days in Great Britain*

Other JMP travel guidebooks by Rick Steves
  Asia Through the Back Door (with Bob Effertz)
  Europe Through the Back Door
  Europe 101: History, Art, and Culture for the Traveler
    (with Gene Openshaw)
  Mona Winks: Self-Guided Tours of Europe's Top Museums
    (with Gene Openshaw)
  2 to 22 Days in Europe
  2 to 22 Days in Great Britain
  2 to 22 Days in Germany, Austria, and Switzerland
  2 to 22 Days in Italy
  2 to 22 Days in Norway, Sweden, and Denmark
  2 to 22 Days in Spain and Portugal
  2 to 22 Days in France (with Steve Smith)

Thanks to my eternal travel partner, research assistant, and wife, Anne. Thanks also to Roy Nicholls, Jodi Burgess, and Dave Hoerlein for their research help, to our well-traveled readers for their input, and to the British friends listed in this book who make a visit to Britain so much more than a series of palaces, museums, and Big Bens.

John Muir Publications, P.O. Box 613, Santa Fe, NM 87504

ISSN 1058-6105
ISBN 1-56261-132-1

Distributed to the book trade by
W. W. Norton & Company, Inc.
New York, New York

Cover Photo Leo de Wys/Sharpe
Maps Dave Hoerlein
Editing Risa Laib
Typography Britt Gallagher
Printer Banta Company

CONTENTS

HOW TO USE THIS BOOK

This book organizes Britain into an efficient, enjoyable, and diverse 22-day adventure. It's a tour guide in your pocket. It lets you be the boss by giving you the best 2,000 miles and 22 days in Britain and suggestions on how to use your limited time and money most efficiently.

2 to 22 Days in Great Britain is for do-it-yourselfers who like the organization and smoothness of a tour without the straitjacket. It's having your scone and eating it, too. This plan offers maximum thrills per mile, minute, and pence. It's designed for travel by rental car but adaptable to train. The pace, fast but not hectic, is designed for the American with limited time who wants to see everything but doesn't want the "if it's Wednesday this must be Warwick" craziness. The plan includes the predictable "required" biggies (such as Big Ben, Stratford, Wordsworth's cottage, and bagpipes in Edinburgh), while mixing in a good dose of "Back Door" intimacy—cozy Cotswold villages, Gaelic folk pubs, angelic boys' choirs, and windswept Roman lookouts.

2 to 22 Days in Great Britain is balanced and streamlined to include only the most exciting castles and churches. To avoid tourist burnout, I've been very selective. We won't visit both Oxford and Cambridge—just Cambridge, the better choice. Of course, that's only my opinion. But after 12 busy years of travel writing, lecturing, and tour guiding, I've developed a sixth sense for what tickles the traveler's fancy. I love this itinerary. It'll knock your spots off.

Of course, connect-the-dots travel isn't perfect, just as color-by-number painting isn't good art. But this book is your smiling Scotsman, your bobby in a bind, your handbook. It's your well thought out and tested itinerary. I've done it—and refined it—many times on my own and with groups. Use it, take advantage of it, but don't let it rule you.

Read this book before you begin your trip. Use it as a rack to hang more ideas on. As you plan, study, travel,

and talk to people, you'll fill the margins with notes. It's
your tool. The book is flexible, with 22 rearrangeable
units (days), each built with these sections:

1. **Introductory overview** for the day.

2. An hour-by-hour **Suggested Schedule** recommended
for that day.

3. A list of the most important **Sightseeing Highlights**
rated: ▲▲▲ Don't miss; ▲▲ Try hard to see; ▲ Worthwhile if you can make it; (no rating) Worth knowing
about.

4. **Transportation** tips and instructions.

5. **Food and Accommodations**: How and where to
find the best budget places, including addresses, phone
numbers, and my favorites.

6. **Orientation** and an easy-to-read map locating recommended places.

7. **Helpful Hints** on shopping, transportation, day-to-
day chores.

8. **Itinerary Options** for those with more or less than
the suggested time, or with particular interests. This itinerary is rubbery!

Dave Hoerlein knows a good map is worth a thousand
words. His maps make my text easy to follow. Dave
points out all major landmarks, streets, and accommodations mentioned in the book and indicates the best city
entry and exit routes for our 22-day plan. His maps are
clear, concise, and readable, but are designed only to orient and direct you until you pick up more detailed maps
at tourist information offices.

In the Appendix, you'll find special sections on English
history and politics and Ireland, as well as BritRail information and a telephone directory.

Cost

This trip's cost breaks down like this: a round-trip U.S.A.-
London flight, $600-$1,000 (depending on the season and
the city you fly from); a three-week car rental (split
between two people, including tax, insurance, and gas) or
three weeks of rail and bus travel, $450; for room and

board, figure $60 a day, double occupancy, for a total of $1,300 per person. This is more than feasible, and if necessary, you can travel cheaper (see my book *Europe Through the Back Door*, Santa Fe, NM: John Muir Publications, 1994, for the skills, tricks, and thrills of traveling cheap). Add $400 or $500 fun money and you've got yourself a great British adventure for around $3,000.

The 2 to 22 Days Accommodations Description Code

I've described my recommended hotels and B&Bs with a standard code. The prices are for one-night stays in peak season, include a hearty English breakfast, and assume you're going direct and not through a tourist information office. Prices may be soft for off-season and longer stays.

S - Single room, or price for one person in a double.

D - Room for two people. (I specify double- and twin-bedded rooms only if they are priced differently, or if a place has only one or the other.)

T - Three-person room (often a double bed with a single).

Q - Four-person room (adding an extra child's bed to a T is usually cheaper).

B - *En suite* room which, in Britain, has a toilet and a shower (most likely) or bath. All rooms have a sink. Any room without a B has access to a free B on the corridor.

W.C. - Toilet in the room. I add this only when a hotel has a three-tiered price system. Otherwise, rooms with a B normally have a W.C.

CC - Accepts credit cards: V=Visa, M=Mastercard, A=American Express. With no CC mention, assume they accept only cash.

No smoking - While most places allow smoking in the rooms and not in the breakfast room, many are now going smoke-free. I'll note these, as well as places that smell musty.

Family deal - Indicates that parents with young children can easily get a room with an extra child's bed or a discount for larger rooms.

Elevator - Almost every place has three floors of rooms, steep stairs, and no elevator. If you're concerned about stairs, call and ask.

According to this code, a couple staying at a "DB-£30, CC-VM" hotel would pay a total of £30 a night for a room with a toilet and shower (or bath). Breakfast is included. The hotel accepts Visa, Mastercard or cash. Since no other type of room is mentioned, the hotel has only DBs (*en suite* two-person rooms).

Prices and Times

I list prices in pounds (£) throughout the book. To keep things simple, I haven't listed all "concessions," which is what the British call discounts for seniors (over 60), youths (16-23), students, and families. Nearly every place charging admission offers concessions. Prices, as well as hours, telephone numbers, and so on, are accurate as of late 1993. Inflation is running at well under 10 percent and the much-discussed recession is keeping prices from rising much. Britain sticks to its schedule (pronounced "shed-jool") better than most European countries, but double-check hours and times when you arrive. The hours listed are for peak season. During off-season, many places close an hour earlier, and some places are open only on weekends or closed entirely in the winter. Confirm your sightseeing plans locally—especially when traveling between October and May.

Money

The British pound sterling (£) is broken into 100 pence (p). A pound, or "quid," is worth about $1.50. Pence means "cents." You'll find coins ranging from 1 pence to £1 and bills from £5 to £50. Multiply the British prices by 1.5 to figure pounds into dollars. £6 is $9, £4.50 is about $7, and 80p is $1.20.

Scotland and Ireland have their own currencies. English and Scottish money are worth the same and are good in both countries (but it can be troublesome to spend Scottish currency in England). The Irish-English money relationship is like the Canadian-American one. English money is a little more valuable. Ireland is a different country—treat it that way.

Britain's 17.5 percent sales tax, the "value added tax" or VAT, is built into nearly everything you buy. Tourists can get a refund on this VAT on souvenirs they take out of the country, but it's often a major headache. Unless you buy something worth several hundred dollars, your refund won't be worth the delays, incidental expenses, and headaches that complicate the lives of TISVATR (Tourists in Search of VAT Refunds).

Even in jolly old England you should use traveler's checks and a money belt. Theft is a part of tourism and the careless are sitting ducks. A money belt (see Catalog) is peace of mind. You can carry lots of cash safely in a money belt.

Many traveling exclusively in Great Britain buy traveler's checks in pounds sterling. While policies vary, some British banks favor various traveler's checks by waiving the commission fee charged (Barclays checks at Barclays banks, American Express checks at Lloyds banks, Thomas Cook checks at Midland banks or Cook offices). But don't let this cloud your assessment of that bank's exchange rates. Save time and money by changing plenty of money at a time. (Banks' charges often exceed £3.) On my last trip, I bought all my pounds in cash from a good American foreign exchange service, stowed them safely in my moneybelt, and never needed a British bank.

Credit cards are not very widely accepted in Britain. I bring a credit card only because it's necessary for renting a car. Spend cash, not plastic, as you travel. If you'll be getting cash advances on your credit card, you'll find that Barclays, National Westminster, and places displaying an Access or Eurocard sign accept MasterCard. Visa is accepted at Barclays and Midland banks.

While Americans have an easy time in Britain with weights and measures (miles, inches, pounds, and ounces), the British now use centigrade in temperatures. British gallons and pints are 20 percent bigger than ours.

Travel Smart
This itinerary assumes you are a well-organized traveler who lays departure groundwork on arrival in a town,

reads a day ahead in this book, visits the local tourist information offices, uses the telephone for reservations and confirmations, and enjoys the hospitality of the British people. Ask questions. Most locals are eager to point you in their idea of the right direction. Carry a phone card, wear a money belt, pack along a pocket-size notebook to organize your thoughts, and practice the virtue of simplicity. If you insist on being confused, your trip will be a mess. Those who expect to travel smart, do.

Scheduling

Your overall itinerary is a fun challenge. Read through this book and note festivals, colorful market days, and days that sights are closed. Sundays have pros and cons as they do for travelers in the U.S.A. (special events, limited hours, closed shops and banks, limited public transportation, no rush hours). Saturdays are virtually weekdays. Popular places are even more popular on weekends—especially sunny weekends, which are sufficient cause for an impromptu holiday in the soggy British Isles.

It's good to alternate intense and relaxed periods. Every trip (and every traveler) needs at least a few slack days. I followed the biblical "one in seven" idea religiously on my last trip.

Bank holidays bring most businesses to a grinding halt on Christmas, December 26, New Year's Day, Good Friday, Easter, the first and last Mondays in May, and the last Monday in August.

To give you a little rooted-ness, I've minimized one-night stands. Staying two nights in the same place, even with hectic travel days before and after, makes for a less grueling trip than changing accommodations daily. One-night stands are less of a problem if you travel in the off-season.

The suggested day-plans, although realistic, are fast, and those who want to have more of a vacation than a busy-bee experience have my hearty blessing to slow down and see less in a more relaxed way. I wish everyone had 30 days to do this 22-day tour.

When to Go

July and August are peak season—my favorite time—with the best weather and the busiest schedule of tourist fun. But peak season is crowded and more expensive than travel in other seasons. This book tackles peak season problems, especially those of finding a room. Travel during "shoulder season" (May, early June, September, and early October) is easier. Shoulder season travelers get minimal crowds, decent weather, the full range of sights and tourist fun spots, and the joy of being able to just grab a room almost whenever and wherever they like—often at a flexible price. Winter travelers find absolutely no crowds, but sights often close early or entirely. The weather can be cold and dreary, and nightfall will draw the shades on your sightseeing well before dinner time.

In my experience, British weather is reliably unpredictable (but mostly bad), and July and August are not much better than shoulder months. May and June can be lovely. Conditions can change several times in a day, but rarely is the weather extreme. Daily averages throughout the year range between 42 and 70 degrees, and temperatures below 32 or over 80 degrees are cause for headlines. Carry a jacket or sweater even in July. It'll go on and off all day with the sun.

Climate Chart: The chart below gives average daytime temperatures and average number of days with more than a trickle of rain.

	Jan	Feb	Mar	Apr	May	Jun	Jul	Aug	Sep	Oct	Nov	Dec
London	43	44	50	56	62	69	71	71	66	58	51	45
	15	13	11	12	11	11	12	11	13	14	15	15
S. Wales	45	45	50	56	61	68	69	69	65	58	51	46
	18	14	13	13	13	13	14	15	16	16	17	18
York	43	44	49	55	60	67	70	70	65	57	49	45
	17	15	13	13	13	14	15	14	14	15	17	17
Edinburgh	42	43	46	51	56	62	65	64	60	54	48	44
	17	15	15	14	14	15	17	16	16	17	17	18

Recommended Guidebooks

This book is your blueprint for an inexpensive, hassle-free trip. *Use this year's edition.* I tell you, you're crazy to save a few bucks by traveling on old information. To rescue those of you who will invariably travel on a two-year-old edition of this book (and realize your mistake too late), I've sent the latest edition of this book to the lead B&B listings in each town for you to transcribe over breakfast.

If you'll be going beyond my recommended route or wanting more information on the sights, supplement *2 to 22 Days in Great Britain* with a few more guidebooks. I know it hurts to spend $30 or $40 on extra books and maps, but when you consider the money they'll save you and the improvements they'll make in your $3,000 vacation—not buying them would be perfectly penny-wise and £-foolish.

Let's Go: Great Britain and Ireland, written and thoroughly updated annually by Harvard students (new editions come out each January), is a general, low-budget, directory-type guidebook listing a broad range of travel services, accommodations, restaurants, and sights. Get *Let's Go* for information on youth hostels, nightlife, and train travel. It's written for students on low budgets, and even though I'm not a student, I use it every year. This is the best single book for those traveling beyond this book's 22-day route.

For cultural and sightseeing background, the American Express, Michelin and Cadogan guides to London, England and Britain are all good.

Europe Through the Back Door (Santa Fe, NM: John Muir Publications, 1994), my book, gives you the basic skills that make this demanding 22-day plan possible. It has chapters on minimizing jet lag, packing light, driving vs. train travel, finding budget beds without reservations, changing money, theft and the tourist, travel photography, long distance telephoning, Ugly Americanism, traveler's toilet trauma, laundry, and itinerary strategies and techniques. The book also includes chapters on forty exciting nooks and undiscovered crannies that I call "Back Doors." Six of these are in the British Isles.

Mona Winks, by Rick Steves and Gene Openshaw (Santa Fe, NM: John Muir Publications, 1993; see back-of-book catalog), takes you through Europe's twenty most frightening and exhausting museums with fun, easy-to-follow, two-hour self-guided tours. In London, Mona leads the way through the British Museum and the National Gallery.

My PBS television series, *Travels in Europe with Rick Steves*, includes six half-hour shows on Britain and Ireland. These may re-air on your local station and are now available in information-packed videotapes (see Back Door catalog).

Maps to Buy in England: If you're driving, get a road atlas (3 miles to 1 inch) covering all of Britain. Ordnance Survey, AA, and Bartholomew editions are available in tourist information offices, gas stations, and bookstores for about £7. For this itinerary, I'd also pick up much more detailed maps for the Cotswold region, North Wales, Windermere Lake District, West Scotland, and North York Moors.

Tourist Information Centres (TIs)

Virtually every British town has a helpful tourist information center eager to make your visit as smooth and enjoyable as possible. Take full advantage of this service. Arrive (or telephone) with a list of questions and a proposed sightseeing plan for them to confirm and most likely improve upon. Pick up maps, brochures, and walking tour information. I use their room-finding service (expensive local mafia, no opinions) only when all else fails. In London, you can pick up everything you'll need in one stop at the National Tourist Information Centre.

Before your trip, send a postcard requesting general information and any specific information you might need (such as a list of upcoming festivals and the free London and Britain maps) to the British Tourist Authority: 551 5th Ave. #701, New York, NY 10176-0799, tel. (212) 986-2200; 2580 Cumberland Parkway #470, Atlanta, GA 30339, tel. (404) 432-9635; 625 North Michigan Ave #1510, Chicago, IL 60611, tel. (312) 787-0490; or 350 S. Figueroa, Rm. 450, Los Angeles, CA 90071, tel. (213) 628-3525.

Flying to London

Flying to London is your major expense, and a little study can save you a bundle. Fares and regulations on flights to England vary all over the USA. From the East Coast, you can fly cheapest by studying the New York Times travel section, comparing standby and cut-rate prices with the best deal your travel agent can give you. From the West Coast, you can't beat what a good travel agent will sell you. You need an agent who knows and enjoys budget European travel. Read the newspapers, talk to other travelers, but most of all, establish a loyal relationship with a good agent.

London is one of the cheapest European destinations from the States, and if you can avoid summer travel it's even cheaper. Off-season West Coast to London round-trip tickets cost around $500.

By Car or Train?

Cars are best for three or more traveling together (especially families with small kids), packing heavy gear, and scouring the countryside. Train and bus are best for single travelers, city-to-city travelers, and blitz tourists.

My choice for this itinerary is to start and finish the trip by connecting big cities by train (London-Bath, York-Cambridge-London) and exploring the more small-town and rural interior (Bath area-Cotswolds-North Wales-Lake District-Highlands-Edinburgh-Hadrian's Wall) footloose and fancy-free by rental car. Britain's 100 mph train system is best in and out of London, but you'll find that wherever it goes, it goes well. Although this book is geared for the driver, I've included information on public transportation for each day's itinerary.

Car Rental

Car rental for this tour is cheapest if arranged in advance through your hometown travel agent (weekly rate with unlimited mileage, pick up in Bath, drop in Durham, York or Cambridge). It's flexible. You can pick up and drop just about anywhere, any time. If you pick up the car in a smaller city, such as Bath, you'll have an easier time adjusting to driving on the other side of the road. If you drop it off early or keep it longer, you'll be credited or charged at a fair, pro-rated price. Big companies have offices in most cities. (Ask to be picked up at your hotel.) Small local rental companies (such as Terminal Car Rental and Alamo Car Rental) can be cheaper but not as flexible.

The Ford 1.3-liter Escort-category car costs about £30 per week more than the smallest cars but feels better on the motorways and safer on the small roads. For peace of mind, I spring for the CDW insurance (Collision Damage Waiver, about £6 per day), which gives a zero-deductible rather than the standard value-of-the-car "deductible." Remember, minibuses are a great budget way to go for five to nine people.

Driving British
Driving in Britain is basically wonderful—once you remember to stay on the left and after you've mastered the "roundabouts." But be warned: every year, I get a few cards from traveling readers advising me that for them, driving British was very difficult and dangerous. Here are a few random tips.

Your U.S.A. license is all you need. A British Automobile Association membership comes with most rentals. Understand its benefits (such as towing and emergency road service). Gas (petrol) costs about $3 per gallon and is self-serve. Know what octane (star) rating your car takes, push the correct button, and pump away. Seat belts are required by law. Speed limits are 30 mph in town, 70 mph on the motorways, and 60 mph elsewhere. The national sign for 60 mph is a white circle with a black slash. While the motorway flow is much faster, time estimates in this book assume a law-abiding speed. Avoid big cities whenever possible. Most have modern ring roads to skirt the congestion. The shortest distance between any two points is usually the motorway. Road signs can be baffling unless you read them with the help of your map.

Parking is confusing. One yellow line (marked on the pavement) means no parking Monday through Saturday during work hours. Double yellow lines mean no parking at any time. Broken yellow lines mean short stops are okay, but always look for explicit signs or ask a passing passerby.

Even in small towns, parking in Britain can be a royal headache. Rather than fight it, I just pull into the most central and handy car park I can find; follow the big blue "P" signs. I keep a bag of 10p and 20p coins in the ashtray for parking meters. Copy your car key as soon as possible so you won't get locked out and your partner can enjoy access to the car. Buy some Windex for clearer sightseeing.

Telephoning in Britain

Use the telephone routinely. You can make long distance calls direct and easily, and there's no language barrier. Call ahead to reserve or reconfirm rooms, check opening hours, confirm tour schedules, and reserve theater tickets. I call home rather than mess with postcards.

The British telephone system is great. Easy-to-find public phone booths are either coin- or card-operated. Newer phones ingeniously take any coin from 10p to £1, and a display shows how your money supply's doing. Only completely unused coins will be returned, so put in biggies with caution. The new and ever more prevalent telephone card is wonderfully convenient. Buy £2, £4, or £10 phone cards at newsstands, hotels, tourist offices, or post offices and use them for ease and economy. Ignore the Mercury phone booths and stick with the dominant British Telecom system.

The only tricky phones you'll use are the expensive Mickey-Mouse coin-op ones in bars and B&Bs. Some require money before you dial and others only after you've connected. Many have a button you must push before you begin talking. But all have clear instructions Long distance in Britain is most expensive from 8:00 a.m.-1:00 p.m., cheaper from 1:00-6:00 p.m., and cheapest from 6:00 p.m.-8:00 a.m. A short call across the country is quite inexpensive. Don't hesitate to call long-distance.

To call long-distance, you'll need the correct area code. Britain has about as many area codes as we have prefixes. For local calls, just dial the three- to seven-digit number. For long-distance ("trunk") calls, you'll find area codes listed by city on phone booth walls, from directory assistance (free and happy to help, dial 142 in London, 192 outside of London), and throughout this book. For a telephone directory, see the Appendix.

To call Britain from another country, replace the beginning zero of the area code with the country code. For instance, Britain's country code is 44 and London's area code is 071. My London B&B's number is 727-7725. To call it from New York, I dial 011 (the U.S.A.'s international code), 44 (Britain's country code), 71 (London's area code without the 0), 727-7725. To call it from old York, dial 071/727-7725.

Note: London's old area code (01) has been replaced by 071 for downtown London (nearly everything we'll hit) and 081 for suburban London.

To call the U.S.A. from Britain, I dial 010 (Britain's international code), 1 (U.S.A.'s country code), 206 (my Seattle area code), and the seven-digit number. Calling the U.S.A. from Britain usually costs over double the U.S.A.-to-Britain rate. But if you use a "USA Direct" service, you'll be charged the lower U.S.A.-to-Britain rate, plus a $2.50 service fee. You'll save money on calls of 3 minutes or more. For 10p, you can actually call home for 5 seconds—long enough to say "call me," or to make sure an answering machine is off so you can call back, using your USA Direct card to connect with a person. USA Direct services are offered by Sprint, AT&T, and MCI (listed in Appendix).

Sleeping in Britain

Thank God Britain has such lousy hotels, because the bed-and-breakfast alternative gives you double the cultural intimacy for half the price.

On this trip, I'm assuming you have a reasonable but limited budget. Skip hotels. Go the B&B way. In this edition I've radically expanded and improved my accommodations listings. If you can use a telephone, speak English, and plan to follow this route, you'll enjoy homey, friendly, clean rooms at a great price by sticking to my listings.

Off this 22-day route, you'll find B&Bs where you need them. Any town with tourists has a tourist office that can book a room for you or give you a list and point you in the right direction. In the absence of a TI, ask people on the street for help.

B&Bs range from large guest houses with 15 to 20 rooms to small homes renting out a spare bedroom. The philosophy of the management determines the character of a place more than its size. Try to avoid places run as a business by absentee owners. My top listings are run by couples who enjoy welcoming the world to their breakfast table. Small places (with a gross income of under £35,000) don't have to pay a 17.5 percent tax and offer cheaper prices. Small places can also skimp on safety regulations and operate even cheaper.

You'll pay £10 to £25 for a B&B in 1994 ($15 to $40 per person). This includes a "full English breakfast." How much coziness, tea, and biscuits are tossed in varies tremendously.

The B&Bs I've recommended are nearly all stocking-feet comfortable and very "homely," as they say in England. My prerequisites for recommending a place are that it must be: friendly; in a central, safe, quiet neighborhood; clean, with good beds and a sink in the room and shower down the hall; a good value; not mentioned in other guidebooks (therefore, filled mostly by English travelers); and willing to hold a room until 4:00 p.m. or so without a deposit (though more and more places are requiring a deposit or credit card number). In certain cases, my recommendations don't meet all these prerequisites. I'm more impressed by a handy location and a fun-loving philosophy than a checklist of facilities.

I promised the owners of the places I list that you will be reliable when you make a telephone reservation; please don't let them (or me) down. If you'll be delayed or won't make it, simply call in. Americans are notorious for "standing up" B&Bs. Being late is no problem if you are in telephone contact.

A few tips: B&B proprietors are selective as to whom they invite in for the night. Risky-looking people (especially two or more single men) find many places suddenly full. If you'll be staying for more than one night you are a "desirable." Sometimes staying several nights earns you a better price—ask about it. If you book through a TI, it'll take a 10 percent commission. If you book direct, the B&B gets it all (and you'll have a better chance of getting a discount). Nearly all B&Bs have plenty of stairs. Expect good exercise and be happy you packed light. If one B&B is full, ask for guidance. (Mentioning this book can help.) Owners usually work together and can call up an ally to land you a bed. "Twin" means two single beds, and "double" means one double bed. If you'll take either one, let them know or you might be needlessly turned away. Every room has a sink. More and more are going *en suite*, meaning with a private shower/tub and W.C. Many better places have a basic room (with a shower down the hall) that they don't even advertise.

B&Bs are not hotels. If you want to ruin your relationship with your hostess, treat her like a hotel staff person. Americans often assume they'll get new towels each day. The British don't, and neither will you. Hang them to dry and reuse.

The British Tourist Board rates hotels and B&Bs with a crown system. B&Bs are rated as follows: no crowns (basic, clean, one bath per 12 people, safe); one crown (no nylon bed linen, a sink in the room, one bath per eight people); two crowns (tea and coffee in room on request, TV in room or lounge, luggage help); three crowns (hot evening meals, one-third of rooms with bathroom); four crowns (three-fourths of rooms with bathroom, nearly a hotel); five crowns (all with private bathroom, valet, porters, virtually a high-class hotel). Some idealistic guest-house proprietors are refusing to bow to the pressure to fill their B&Bs with all the gimmicks and extras. They continue to offer just a good bed with a shower down the hall, traditional breakfast, and a warm welcome. They go unlisted, but are an excellent value. In the First World, simplicity is subversive.

Realizing that the facilities-based crown system was too impersonal, the tourist board added a rating measuring the cozy, personal, intangible touches (commended, highly commended, deluxe). While I don't worry much about either rating, coziness is more important than crowns.

While you can do this tour any time of year without reservations, it's best to call ahead and nail down rooms in my best listings as soon as you can say when you'll be there and don't mind the commitment. Generally a phone call with a promise to reconfirm a day in advance will hold a room. Many places will ask for a credit card number or a traveler's check and send you a map and confirmation letter. Given the high stakes, erratic B&B values, and the quality of the gems I've found for this book, I'd highly recommend calling ahead for rooms (before your trip or at least 3 days in advance as you travel).

Youth Hostels: Britain has 400 youth hostels of all shapes and sizes. They can be historic castles or depressing huts, serene and comfy or overrun by noisy children. Unfortunately, they have become over-priced and, in general, I can no longer recommend them unless you're on a very tight budget and want to cook your own meals or if you're traveling with a group that doesn't have much money and likes to sleep on bunk beds in big rooms. If you're traveling alone, hosteling is the best way to defeat hotel loneliness. Hostels are also a tremendous source of local and budget travel information. If you hostel selectively, you'll enjoy historical and very interesting buildings.

Anyone can hostel in Britain. If you don't have a hostel card, you can get a one-night guest membership for £1.50. If you plan to hostel, use the excellent British hostel guidebook, available at any hostel.

Eating in Britain
I don't mind English food. But then, I liked dorm food, too. True, England isn't famous for its cuisine and probably never will be, but we tourists have to eat. If there's any good place to cut corners to stretch your budget in Britain, it's in eating. Here are a few tips on budget eating.

The English (or Scottish or Welsh) "fry" is famous as a hearty way to start the day. Also known as a "heart attack on a plate," the breakfast is especially feasty if you've just come from the land of the skimpy continental breakfast across the Channel. Your standard "fry" gets off to a healthy start with juice and cereal or porridge. (Try Weetabix, a soggy English cousin of shredded wheat. Scotland serves great porridge.) Next, with tea or coffee, you get a heated plate with a fried egg, very lean Canadian-style bacon, a pretty bad sausage, a grilled tomato, and often a slice of delightfully greasy pan toast, baked beans, and sautéed mushrooms. Toast comes on a rack (to cool quickly and crisply) with butter and marmalade. This meal tides many travelers over until dinner. Order only what you'll eat. B&B hostesses tend to be like your mother and don't like to see food wasted.

Many B&Bs don't serve breakfast until 8:30. If you need an early start, ask politely if it's possible. Consider skipping breakfast on occasion if a quick start is important.

Picnicking for lunch saves time and money. Outfit your car with a back-seat cardboard pantry: boxes of orange juice (pure by the liter), fresh bread, tasty English cheese, meat, a tube of Colman's English mustard, local eatin' apples, bananas, small tomatoes, rice crackers, gorp or nuts, chocolate-covered "Digestive Biscuits," and any local specialties. Toss in a plastic water-bottle, disposable cups, paper towels, ziplock baggies, and a Swiss Army knife. At open-air markets and supermarkets, you can easily get food in small quantities. (Three little tomatoes and two bananas cost me 40p.) Decent sandwiches (£1.50) are sold everywhere. I often munch "meals on wheels" en route (or on a bus or boat tour) to save 30 precious minutes and enjoy a relaxed meal while driving.

Although British restaurants are fairly expensive, there are plenty of cheap alternatives: fish-and-chips joints, Chinese and Indian take-outs, cafeterias, pubs (see below), B&Bs that serve evening meals, and your typical, good old greasy-spoon cafés. Bakeries have meat pies, pastries, yogurt and cartons of "semi-skimmed" milk—ideal for fresh, fast, cheap lunches.

Pub Grub and Beer

Pubs are a basic part of the British social scene, and whether you're a teetotaler or a beer-guzzler, they should be a part of your travel here. Pub is short for "public house." It's an extended living room where, if you don't mind the stickiness, you can feel the pulse of Britain. Most traditional atmospheric pubs are in the countryside and smaller towns. Unfortunately, many city pubs have been afflicted with an excess of brass, ferns, and video games. In any case, smart travelers use the pubs to eat, drink, get out of the rain, and make new friends.

Pub grub, which is getting better each year, is far and away Britain's best eating value. For £5, you'll get a basic budget hot lunch or dinner in friendly surroundings. The Good Pub Guide, published annually by the British Consumers Union, is excellent. I recommend certain pubs, but food can spoil, and your B&B host usually takes pride in being right up-to-date on the best neighborhood pub grub. Ask for advice.

Pubs generally serve assorted meat pies (such as steak and kidney pie, shepherd's pie), curried dishes, fish, quiche, vegetables, and invariably chips and peas. Servings are hearty, service is quick, and you'll rarely spend more than £4 to £6 ($6-$9). Your beer or cider adds another dollar or two. Free tap water is always available. A "ploughman's lunch" is a modern "traditional English meal" that nearly every tourist tries . . . once. Eat at pubs that advertise their food and are crowded with locals. Some pubs still serve only lousy microwaved snacks.

The British take great pride in their beer. They think that drinking beer cold and carbonated, as Americans do, ruins the taste. At pubs, long "hand pulls" are used to pull the traditional rich-flavored "real ales" up from the cellar. These are the connoisseur's favorites: fermented naturally, varying from sweet to bitter, often with a hoppy or nutty flavor. Notice the fun names. Experiment with the obscure local micro-brews. Short "hand pulls" at the bar mean colder and fizzier mass-produced and less interesting keg beers. Mild beers are sweeter with a creamy malt flavoring. Stout is dark and more bitter, like Guinness. For a cold, refreshing, basic American-style beer, ask for a "lager." Try the draft cider . . . carefully. English ladies like a half-beer and half-lemonade "shandy." Teetotalers can order a soft drink. Drinks are served by the pint or the half-pint. (It's almost feminine for a man to order just a half; I order mine with quiche.) Don't wait to be served. Jostle right up to the bar and pay as you're served. Don't tip (unless you've drunk way too much).

Pub hours vary. The strictly limited wartime hours were finally ended a few years ago, and now pubs can serve beer from 11:00 a.m. to 11:00 p.m., and Sunday from noon to 10:30 p.m. Children are served food and soft drinks in pubs, but you must be 18 to order a beer. People go to a "public house" to be social. They want to talk. Pubs are the next best thing to relatives in every town.

Ugly Americanism
We travel all the way to Great Britain to experience something different—to become temporary locals. Americans have a knack for finding certain truths to be God-given and self-evident—such as cold beer; a bottomless coffee cup; long, hot showers; and driving on the right-hand side of the road. One of the beauties of travel is the opportunity to see that there are logical, civil, and even better alternatives. If there is a British image of you and me, we are big, loud, aggressive, impolite, rich, and a bit naive. The American worker earns twice the salary of his British counterpart, yet taxes, unemployment, and the cost of living are all higher for the British worker.

Still, I find warmth and friendliness throughout Great Britain. An eagerness to go local ensures that I enjoy a full dose of British hospitality.

Europeans, in general, admire and support a strong America. The British like us even though many will remind us that our high-flying national eagle is not perfectly house-trained. While Europeans look bemusedly at some of our Yankee excesses—and worriedly at others—they nearly always afford us individual travelers all the warmth we deserve.

Freedom

This book's goal is to free you, not chain you. Please defend your spontaneity as you would your mother. Use this book to sort Britain's galaxy of sights into the most interesting, representative, diverse, and efficient 22 days of travel. Use it to avoid time- and money-wasting mistakes, and to get more intimate with Britain by traveling without a tour—as a temporary local. This book is a point of departure from which you can shape your best possible travel experience. Only a real dullard would do this entire tour exactly as I've laid it out. Personalize! Anyone who has read this far has what it takes intellectually to do this tour on his or her own. Be confident and militantly positive; relish the challenge and rewards of your own planning.

Send Me a Postcard, Drop Me a Line

Although I do what I can to keep this book accurate and up to date, Britain refuses to stand still. If you enjoy a successful trip with the help of this book and would like to share your discoveries, please send your tips, recommendations, criticisms, witticisms, or corrections to Rick Steves, 109 4th Avenue North, Box 2009, Edmonds, WA 98020. Your feedback is my favorite mail. To share tips or to get an update of this book before your trip, tap into our free computer bulletin board travel information service (206-771-1902:1200 or 2400/8/N/1). All correspondents will receive a 2-year subscription to our Back Door Travel quarterly newsletter (it's free anyway).

Now, raise your travel dreams to their upright and locked position, and fly into the best British vacation you can imagine!

BACK DOOR TRAVEL PHILOSOPHY
AS TAUGHT IN *EUROPE THROUGH THE BACK DOOR*

Travel is intensified living—maximum thrills per minute and one of the last great sources of legal adventure. Travel is freedom. It's recess, and we need it.

Experiencing the real Europe requires catching it by surprise, going casual . . . "Through the Back Door."

Affording travel is a matter of priorities. (Make do with the old car.) You can travel—simple, safe, and comfortable—anywhere in Europe for $50 a day plus transportation costs. In many ways, spending more money only builds a thicker wall between you and what you came to see. Europe is a cultural carnival, and time after time, you'll find that its best acts are free and the best seats are the cheap ones.

A tight budget forces you to travel close to the ground, meeting and communicating with the people, not relying on service with a purchased smile. Never sacrifice sleep, nutrition, safety, or cleanliness in the name of budget. Simply enjoy the local-style alternatives to expensive hotels and restaurants.

Extroverts have more fun. If your trip is low on magic moments, kick yourself and make things happen. If you don't enjoy a place, maybe you don't know enough about it. Seek the truth. Recognize tourist traps. Give people the benefit of your open mind. See things as different, but not better or worse. Any culture has much to share.

Of course, travel, like the world, is a series of hills and valleys. Be fanatically positive and militantly optimistic. If something's not to your liking, change your liking. Travel is addicting. It can make you a happier American as well as a citizen of the world. Our Earth is home to nearly six billion equally important people. It's humbling to travel and find that people don't envy Americans. They like us, but with all due respect, they wouldn't trade passports.

Globe-trotting destroys ethnocentricity. It helps you understand and appreciate different cultures. Travel changes people. It broadens perspectives and teaches new ways to measure quality of life. Many travelers toss aside their hometown blinders. Their prized souvenirs are the strands of different cultures they decide to knit into their own character. The world is a cultural yarn shop. And Back Door travelers are weaving the ultimate tapestry. Come on, join in!

DAY 1 Arrive in London, visit the tourist information office to lay the groundwork for the next three weeks, get set up in your B&B, blow through London on the open deck of a double-decker orientation tour bus and take an evening pinch-me-I'm-in-Britain walk through downtown.

DAYS 2, 3, and **4** It takes three days to explore the highlights of London. Essential experiences are the Beefeater tour of the Tower of London with an ogle at the greatest crown jewels on earth, hearing the chimes of Big Ben, seeing the Halls of Parliament in action, hob-nobbing with the tombstones in Westminster Abbey, ducking WWII bombs in Churchill's underground Cabinet War Rooms, overfeeding the pigeons at Trafalgar Square, visiting with Leonardo, Botticelli, and Rembrandt in the newly renovated National Gallery, whispering across the dome of St. Paul's Cathedral, and rummaging through our civilization's attic at the British Museum. Then you'll enjoy some of Europe's best people-watching at Covent Gardens, the Buckingham Palace Changing of the Guard, the earth-shaking Imperial War Museum, the new Museum of the Moving Image, and a cruise down the Thames River. Spend one evening at a theater or concert hall and the others catching your breath. End Day 4 with a 75-minute train ride to your B&B in Bath.

DAY 5 Tour Bath's Roman and medieval mineral baths before taking a coffee break in the elegant Pump Room. Follow a local guide for a 2-hour walking tour through the fascinating highlights of England's trend-setting Old World Hollywood. Spend the afternoon browsing and touring England's greatest collection of costumes—300 years of fashion history, from Anne Boleyn to Twiggy.

DAY 6 Pick up your rental car in Bath for a side-trip to explore Avebury, every Druid's favorite stone circle; mystical Glastonbury, home of Avalon, King Arthur, and the

Holy Grail; and Wells, with its medieval center and striking cathedral. After a music-filled evensong service in
the cathedral and a pub dinner, head home to Bath.

DAY 7   Drive into Wales, through its capital of Cardiff,
and to the Welsh Folk Museum, a park full of restored
old houses, offering an intimate look at this fascinating
culture. After a scenic drive past evocative Tintern
Abbey, set up at Stow-on-the-Wold or Chipping Campden in the heart of the Cotswold Hills.

DAY 8   Spend half the day in the thatch-happy
Cotswold Hills, savoring the most delicious of England's
villages, the quintessence of quaint. Then visit Blenheim
Palace.

DAY 9   After a morning in Shakespeare's hometown,
Stratford, tour England's finest medieval castle at Warwick and drive through England's industrial storm (Birmingham) to its industrial birthplace, the Ironbridge
Gorge.

DAY 10   Today is devoted to the birthplace of the
Industrial Revolution. In the Ironbridge Gorge on the
Severn River, you'll find a series of museums that take
the visitor back into those heady days when Britain was
racing into the modern age and pulling the rest of the
West with her. Then it's into the romantic beauty of
North Wales, setting up in Ruthin.

DAY 11   Circling scenic and historic North Wales, spin
through a woolen mill, the Caernarfon Castle, awesome
Mount Snowdon, and a bleak slate mine, arriving home
in time to indulge in a medieval Welsh banquet complete with harp, singing wenches, mead, daggers, and
bibs.

DAY 12   From Edenism to Hedonism, drive from idyllic
North Wales to Blackpool, England's Coney Island.
Britain's most popular tourist attraction—which nearly all

Americans skip—is 6 miles of fortune-tellers, fish-and-chips, amusement piers, beaches, warped mirrors, and hordes of Englanders. It's recess and time to put on a hat with a built-in ponytail!

DAY 13   For another splash of contrast, drive into the pristine Lake District, where Wordsworth's poems still shiver in trees and ripple on ponds. After a short cruise and a 6-mile walk around the loveliest of these lovely lakes, check into a remote farmhouse B&B.

DAY 14   Pick up your poetic license at Wordsworth's famous Dove Cottage. This is a free day to relax, recharge, and take the hike you like, maybe even write a poem.

DAY 15   Steam north into Scotland, past bustling Glasgow, along the scenic Loch Lomond, for a 6-hour drive to the Highlands. Blaring bagpipes and swirling kilts accompany dinner tonight in Oban, the "gateway to the Hebrides."

DAY 16   Today's all-day joyride features the stark beauty of Glencoe, a drive from coast to coast along the Caledonian Canal, and Loch Ness. While you may not see the monster, you'll tour a grand castle and enjoy some fine Highland scenery. After a visit to Culloden, where the English finally defeated Bonnie Prince Charlie and his Scottish hopes, zip down from Inverness to Edinburgh.

DAY 17   Edinburgh, the colorful city of Robert Louis Stevenson, Walter Scott, and Robert Burns, is one of Europe's most entertaining cities. Hike the Royal Mile, touring the Edinburgh Castle, the Holyrood Palace—where the queen stays when she's in town—and everything in between.

DAY 18   Climb to the top of the Walter Scott Memorial for a royal view of the Royal Mile. Then climb back 200 years into Georgian England with a walk through the New

Town. Enjoy a concert in the park, the best shopping in Scotland, and an evening of music and folk-dancing.

DAY 19 Two hours south of Edinburgh, Hadrian's Wall reminds us that Britain was an important Roman colony 2,000 years ago. After a walk along the ramparts and through a fine Roman museum, it's on to Durham for a float through Britain's greatest Romanesque (Norman) cathedral. An evensong service here takes you a thousand years back and a thousand miles up.

DAY 20 Spend the morning in the year 1900 at the Beamish Open-Air museum, in James Herriot country, or wandering lost in the lonesome North York Moors with their time-passed villages, bored sheep, and powerful landscapes. Turn in your rental car and set up in the city of York in time to enjoy an introductory walking tour led by an old Yorker.

DAY 21 York has three world-class museums and the finest Gothic church in England. Divide this day between the great York Minster, the Jorvik exhibit (the best Viking museum anywhere), Europe's greatest railroad museum, and the York Castle Museum—a walk with Charles Dickens.

DAY 22 Spend midday checking out the town, colleges, and art of Cambridge. With its sleepy river, lush green grounds, mellow study halls, and old streets clogged with bicycles, Cambridge is worth all the time you can muster before catching the hour-long train ride into London. The circle is complete, and you've experienced the best 22 days Britain has to offer. Blimey, next year you might want 22 more.

Itinerary Options: Consider going directly from London's airport to Bath, an easier place to get over jet lag. Finish your trip in London with a side trip to Cambridge. It is difficult to enjoy a place on your first or second night in Europe. (This important option is discussed more on Day 1.)

Also, many people save two days and a lot of miles by going directly from the Lake District to Edinburgh, skipping the long drive through Scotland. These two days can be put to good use slowing down a plan that for many is too fast.

While I've considered Wales rather than Scotland or Ireland the best quick look at Celtic Britain, you could splice Ireland in or tack it on to the end of your trip as discussed in the Appendix chapter on Ireland.

FLY TO LONDON

On this busy first day, you'll fly halfway round the world, then set up and settle in for a night in one of Europe's most exciting cities—London.

Suggested Schedule

Depart U.S.A.

Arrive at airport in London and visit airport's London tourist office. Travel downtown, following "Arrival in London" instructions carefully.

Check into your hotel or B&B.

Make trip-organizing phone calls from your hotel.

Take the "Original London Transport Sightseeing Tour" for a quick once-over of the city.

Ride the bus downtown to Westminster Bridge for your first night walk.

You must stay awake until 10:00 p.m.

Flying Away
Call the airport before leaving home to be sure your plane's on schedule. Combat boredom and frustration from the inevitable delays and long lines by bringing something to do—a book, a journal, darts, or some hand-work. If you haven't already carefully read this book from cover to cover, do so, making notes during the flight. Expect delays and remember that no matter how long it takes, flying to England is a very easy, space-age way to get there. Don't be unreasonable in your expectations. If you land safely on the day you hope to, it's been a smashing success.

To minimize jet lag
■ Leave well rested. Schedule a false departure day one day early. Plan accordingly and, even at the cost of hecticity the day before, enjoy a peaceful last day.

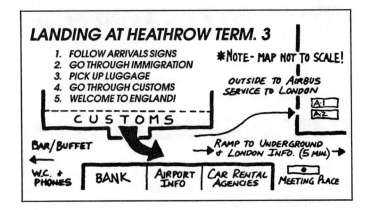

■ During the flight, minimize stress by eating lightly, avoiding alcohol, caffeine, and sugar. Drink juice. ("Two glasses of orange juice, no ice please.") Take walks.

■ Sleep through the in-flight movie—or at least close your eyes and fake it (unless you're reading this book).

■ Change your watch (and your mind) to London time. Upon arrival, get exercise, daylight, and fresh air.

Arrival in London

When you fly to Europe, you lose a day. If you leave on Friday, you land on Saturday. From the airplane, follow the "arrivals" signs to baggage and customs. Heathrow Airport is user-friendly. Read signs, ask questions. Collect your baggage and be waved through customs.

After customs, you'll pop into throngs of waiting loved ones. You'll see a bank (open 24 hours daily, not great rates) and the airport terminal's information desk. Change some money, and buy a *Time Out* or *What's On* entertainment monthly at the newsstand. At the information desk, pick up a London map, ask about your necessary transportation connection, and get directions to Heathrow's tourist office (TI). You could also drop by your car rental agency's desk to confirm your pick-up plans. Then follow signs to the "underground" to reach the TI. (This is a long, but worthwhile walk. If you're planning to ride the Airbus into London, leave your partner at the terminal with your bags.) Heathrow's TI (daily 9:00 a.m.-6:00 p.m.) gives you

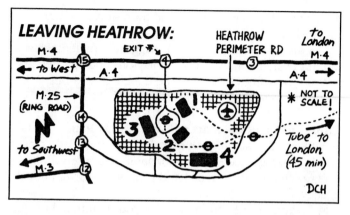

all the help that London's Victoria Station does, with none of the crowds. Consider buying a Heritage pass (discount ticket to many of Britain's top sights), BT phone card, and subway pass (if you're riding the tube into London). Then hop on the London-bound subway or walk back into the airport to catch the Airbus. If you're going to Bath, follow signs to the bus station and catch your National Express bus to Bath.

Anyone flying British Air will land in the new and impressive Terminal 4, which has everything Terminal 3 has except the TI.

Most flights arrive at Heathrow (from the U.S.A., generally before noon), but some (especially charters) go into Gatwick Airport, halfway between London and the southern coast. No problem. Trains shuttle between Gatwick and London's Victoria Station four times an hour (a 30-minute, £8 ride). Phone numbers for the airports and airlines are listed in the Appendix.

Transportation into London from Heathrow
The fastest, easiest, and cheapest way into London is by tube (£2.80, free with £3.70 all-day pass, 14 miles to Victoria station in 45 minutes, departures every 10 minutes) or Airbus (£5, twice an hour, 6:30 a.m.-8:00 p.m., buy ticket on bus, tel. 081/897-3305). All my recommended hotel neighborhoods are on one of the two Airbus lines (A1: South Kensington is third stop, Victoria Station is last stop.

A2: Notting Hill Gate, second and third stops; for Bloomsbury, get off at Russell Square, the last stop).

The tube works fine, but with baggage, I prefer taking the Airbus into London—no connections underground and a lovely view from the top of the double-decker bus. Ask the driver to remind you when to get off.

Things to Do at the Start of Your 22-Day Plan

Whether you're starting your trip in London or Bath, plan ahead, making necessary confirmations and reservations.

■ Confirm your car rental and pick-up plans with rental agency.

■ Reserve your London hotel for your return in three weeks.

■ Reserve tickets for any special concerts or plays that are sold out now, but won't be in three weeks.

■ Book a seat at the Stratford Theater if the Royal Shakespeare Company is playing during your night in the Cotswolds. Tel. 0789/295623.

■ If you'll be attending the Edinburgh Festival (August 14-September 3 in 1994), call the festival office at 031/225-5756 to book a ticket by credit card from April on. And while you're at it, book your Edinburgh room.

■ Specific reservations to make (especially in July and August): (1) Book whatever B&Bs you can now or as soon as you're ready to commit to a date. (2) Book the Ruthin Medieval Banquet, either direct or through a Ruthin B&B. (3) Write to the Tower of London (H. M. Governor, Tower of London, London EC3) three weeks in advance, with an envelope stamped and addressed to your London hotel, requesting an invitation to the moving "ceremony of the keys." Say which night or nights you can come (free).

Radical itinerary option: Start with Bath. Do London at the end of your trip.

This is a big and rather important decision. I actually think that going directly to Bath on the day you land and visiting London at the end of your trip is more efficient. The Britain tours I organize (which do this basic 22-day route) now start in Bath and it works wonderfully.

Issues to consider: Do you want to start or finish with the big-city bang? Bath is a much more gentle town in which to deal with jet lag. You'll be too sleepy to enjoy a London play on evening one or two. There's nothing to stay awake for in Bath. The Heathrow-Bath connection at the start of your trip is easier than the York-Heathrow connection at the end of your trip. After much mental wrestling, I kept London at the beginning of this guidebook (thinking that's the logical place to look for the dominant city). Please give this some thought as you plan your trip. If you do restructure the itinerary (Heathrow-Bath-everything else-York-Cambridge-London-Heathrow), pick up your car as you leave Bath and drop it when you arrive in York.

Transportation to Bath
From Heathrow: National Express buses make the direct 2½ hour trip to Bath about every two hours from Heathrow's Central Bus Station (departures to "Bath Spa" at 10:30, 12:30, 2:30, 4:30, tel. 081/730-0202). By car from Heathrow, simply follow the M4 signs to "West." This is the super-motorway.

   From downtown London: Trains leave Paddington Station every hour (at a quarter after) for the 75-minute ride to Bath. £25 tickets can be bought in advance or on the train from the conductor. Consider the £25 guided bus tour from London to Stonehenge and Bath for the same price, and simply leave it in Bath.

London orientation, sightseeing tour, night walk, and accommodation—see Days 2, 3, and 4.

THE BEST OF LONDON

London, more than 600 square miles of urban jungle with 7 million struggling people, many of whom speak English, is a world in itself, a barrage on all the senses. On my first visit, I felt very, very small. London is much more than its museums and famous landmarks. It's a living, breathing organism that manages to thrive.

The sights of London alone could easily fill a 22-day trip. You'll have three days to enjoy as many of these sights as time, energy, and sanity will allow. (Note: these plans assume you took the orientation bus tour on your arrival day—see London Tours below.)

Suggested Schedule Day 2

9:00	Tower of London (Beefeater tour, crown jewels).
12:00	Picnic on Thames cruising from Tower to Westminster Bridge.
1:00	Big Ben, Halls of Parliament, Westminster Abbey, walk up Whitehall, Cabinet War Rooms.
4:00	Trafalgar Square, National Gallery.
5:30	Visit National Tourist Information Centre at Piccadilly, planning ahead for your trip.
6:30	Dinner near Piccadilly.

Suggested Schedule Day 3

9:00	Spend 30 minutes in a phone booth getting all essential elements of your trip nailed down.
10:00	Museum of London, "The City" of London, and St. Paul's Cathedral. Climb to the top for the view. Many other Wren churches are nearby, as well as the Old Bailey.
1:00	Covent Gardens for lunch and people-watching.
3:00	British Museum, walking tour, or shopping.
7:30	Visitors' Gallery in Houses of Parliament (if in session) or take in a play or concert (if still awake).

Suggested Schedule Day 4	
9:00	Some serious shopping at Harrods or open air markets.
11:30	Changing of the Guard at Buckingham Palace.
1:00	Museum of the Moving Image.
3:00	Imperial War Museum, Tate Gallery, cruise to Greenwich, or early train to Bath.
6:15	Train to Bath.
7:30	Check into B&B in Bath.

London Orientation

London Town has changed dramatically in recent years, and many visitors are surprised to find how "un-English" it is. Whites are now actually a minority in major parts of a city that once symbolized white imperialism. Arabs have nearly bought out the area north of Hyde Park. Chinese take-outs now outnumber fish-and-chips shops (or "fee 'n' chee shops" as some locals call them). Many hotels are run by people with foreign accents, while outlying suburbs are home to huge communities of Indians and Pakistanis. London is learning—sometimes fitfully—to live as a microcosm of its formerly vast empire.

With just three days here, you'll get no more than a quick splash in this teeming human tide pool. But hopefully, with a quick orientation, you'll get a good sampling of its top sights, history, cultural entertainment, and ever-changing human face.

London has all the pitfalls of any big city, but if you're on the ball, informed, and well-organized, it won't cost a fortune, you won't get ripped off, and you'll leave looking forward to your return.

London Information

You can't McGoo London. Study this book. More information on specific slices of London abounds. You can get by with the free London transport and tourist map (available at the TI, some tube stations, and hotels), but the TI's 95p map is as good as the £4 maps sold in newsstands and well worthwhile (free from BTA in the U.S.A: 551 5th Ave. #701, New York, NY, 10176).

London Tourist Information Centres are located at
Heathrow Airport (daily 9:00 a.m.-6:00 p.m., most convenient and least crowded), in Victoria Station (daily 8:00
a.m.-6:00 p.m., shorter hours in winter), at Selfridges
Department Store on Oxford Street, and at Harrods (regular store hours). Just off Piccadilly, the National Tourist
Info Centre (see below), is less crowded and has a
London section. Smelling a new source of profit, London
TIs are no longer answering phones. They're pushing a
50p-per-minute telephone information service. Beware of
the many area code 0839 toll numbers.

Bring your itinerary and a checklist of questions to the
handiest TI office. Go over your London plans, buy a
ticket to a play, save a pound by buying your orientation
bus tour ticket here, and pick up these publications:
London Planner (all hours, monthly), walking tour
brochure, theater guide (bi-weekly), Britain map with
directory of all TIs (99p), the *Quick Guide to London*,
and a London map (95p, free in U.S.A.).

For the best listing of what's happening (plays, movies,
restaurants, concerts, exhibitions, walking tours, protests,
children's activities, and so on), pick up a current copy
of *Time Out* or *What's On* at any newsstand. If you want
theater reviews, *Time Out* is worth the extra 40p. You
can also call 071/222-8070 for a taped rundown on
"Children's London" (Monday-Friday 4:00-6:00 p.m.).

National Tourist Information
The energetic British Tourist Authority's impressive
National Tourist Information Centre, a block downhill
from Piccadilly Circus (12 Regent St., Monday-Friday 9:00
a.m.-6:30 p.m., Saturday and Sunday 10:00 a.m.-4:00
p.m.), has a well-equipped London/England desk, a
Wales desk (tel. 071/409-0969), an all-Ireland desk (tel.
071/839-8416), an extensive travel book and map shop, a
British Rail information desk, and an American Express
Bank (no change fee, decent rates, Sundays too). Use
this place to gather whatever information, maps, and
advice you'll need for your entire trip. So that you can
be well-prepared for each stop on this 22-day plan, I rec-

ommend getting a map for each city you'll visit, and the following:

- ■ *A Britain Road Atlas, AA* or *Ordnance Survey,* £7 (for drivers only)
- ■ *Let's Go: Great Britain and Ireland,* £15 (50% over U.S. price, train travelers only)
- ■ *Youth Hostel Association 1993 Guide,* £3 (hostelers only)
- ■ *Stonehenge and Avebury* (picture book), £2
- ■ *Wales Tourist Map,* £1.50
- ■ *Cotswolds Wyedean Official Tourist Map* (covering Tintern to Coventry), £2.60
- ■ *Lake District Touring Map* (entire region or just the NW corner, Ordnance Survey), £4.30
- ■ *The Michelin Green Guide to Britain,* £7
- ■ *Leisure Touring Map of Scotland,* £2

Yes, this will lighten your money belt by a few pounds, but this information can set you up to really travel smart. You are your own guide. Be a good one.

The Scottish Tourist Centre is a block away (19 Cockspur St., tel. 071/930-8661).

Transportation in London

London's taxis, buses, and subway system make a private car unnecessary. In a city this size, you must get comfortable with its public transportation. Don't be timid; take the bull by the tail, and in no time London will have you by the horns.

Taxis: Big, black, carefully regulated cabs are everywhere. I never met a crabby cabbie in London. They love to talk and know every nook and cranny in town. Rides start at £1 and cost about £1 per tube stop. Often legitimate charges are added on, but for a short ride, three people in a cab travel at tube prices. If a cab's top light is on, just wave it down. If that doesn't work, ask for directions to a nearby taxi stand. Telephoning is unnecessary; taxis are everywhere. Un-metered private taxis can be cheaper than the traditional black cabs, but are much more likely to rip you off.

Buses: London's extensive bus system is easy to follow if you have a map listing the routes. Get a free map from a TI or tube station, or spring for the more-detailed 95p map available at TIs. Signs at stops list routes clearly. Conductors are terse but helpful. Ask to be reminded when it's your stop. Just hop on, take a seat, and relax. (Go upstairs for the best view.) You'll be ticketed whenever the conductor gets around to it. Buses and taxis are miserable during rush hours, 8:00-10:00 a.m. and 4:00-7:00 p.m. Rides start at 90p. Get in the habit of hopping buses for quick little straight shots if you have a transit pass.

The London Underground or "Tube": London's tube is one of this planet's great people-movers. Every city map includes a tube map. Rip one out and keep it in your shirt pocket. You'll need it. Navigate by color-coded lines and north (always up on London maps), south, east, or west. (In fact, think in terms of N, S, E, and W in your general London navigation.) Buy your ticket at the window or from coin-op machines to avoid the line (practice a few fares on the punchboard to see how the system works), then descend to the platform level. You'll need your ticket to leave the system. Many tracks are shared by several lines, and electronic signboards announce which train is next. Each train has its final destination or line name above its windshield. Read the system notices clearly posted on the platforms; they explain the tube's latest flood, construction, or other problems. Ask questions of locals and watch your wallet. Bring something to do to pass the waits productively, especially on the notoriously tardy Circle Line. When leaving the tube, save time by choosing the best street exit (look at the maps on the walls). "Tubing" is by far the fastest long-distance transport in town. Any ride in the Central Zone (on or within the Circle Line, including virtually all my recommended sights and hotels) costs 90p. Remember, "subway" means pedestrian underpass in "English." For tube and bus information, call 222-1234.

London Tube and Bus Passes: There are three handy tube/bus passes to consider: The "Travel Card," covering zones 1 and 2, gives you unlimited travel for a day starting after 9:30 a.m. for £2.60. The "LT Card" offers the same benefits, without the "off peak" restriction, for £3.70. The "7 Day LT Card" costs £9.30, covers zone 1, and requires a passport-type photo (cut one out of any old snapshot and bring it from home). All passes are purchased as easily as a normal ticket from any station, and cover both tube and bus transportation. If you figure you'll take three rides, get the day pass.

Helpful Hints

Theft Alert—Be on guard here more than anywhere in Britain for pickpockets and theft, particularly on public transportation and in places crowded with tourists.

Sunday Activities—Few London sights are open on Sunday before 2:00 p.m. (Major museums are usually open Sunday afternoons.) Some Sunday morning activities: church at St. Paul's or the Tower of London chapel, Original London Sightseeing Tour by bus, a Thames cruise, Imperial War Museum, Museum of the Moving Image, Kew Gardens and Palace, Madame Tussaud's, Victoria and Albert museum (open at noon), Cabinet War Rooms, and open-air markets at Petticoat Lane or Camden Market.

American Express—London's many Amex offices (tel. 930-4411) are open six days a week for mail pickups, seven days a week for money exchange.

Storage—You can leave anything you won't need in a well-labeled bag at your hotel if you'll be returning in three weeks.

Phones/addresses—In London, dial 999 for emergency help and 142 for directory assistance (both calls are free). The area code for any downtown London phone number is 071, for suburban London, 081. Streets are named in segments. The London postal code can be used as a rough compass, with districts numbered SW1, W1, NW6, and so on. The number is a rough measure of the distance from Trafalgar, the city center.

Hello London Walk (ideal for jet lag night)

Enjoy a "very relaxed introduction to London" walk. Catch a bus to Westminster Bridge (#12 from Notting Hill Gate or #211 from Victoria Station). Sit on the top deck and relax

until you get to your stop, the first stop after the bridge.
Walk downstream to Jubilee Promenade for a capital
view, then for that "Wow, I'm really in London!" feeling,
cross the bridge to view the floodlit Houses of Parliament
and Big Ben up close. If you ride the tube, the
Westminster stop is right at Big Ben. Walk halfway across
the bridge for the great view.

To thrill your loved ones (or to bug the envious), call
home from a pay phone near Big Ben at about three minutes before the hour. (You'll find a phone on Great
George Street, across from Parliament Square.) As Big
Ben chimes, stick the receiver outside the booth and
prove you're in London: Ding dong ding dong . . . dong
ding ding dong.

Then cross Whitehall to see the Churchill Statue in the
park. (He's electrified to avoid the pigeon problem that
stains so many other great statues.) Walk up Whitehall
toward Trafalgar Square. Stop at the barricaded and
guarded little Downing Street to see #10, home of the
British prime minister. Break the bobby's boredom—ask
him a question. Just before Trafalgar Square, drop into the
Clarence Pub for a reasonable dinner or pint of whatever
you fancy (cheaper cafeterias and eateries on the same
block or under St. Martin's church on Trafalgar). From
Trafalgar, walk to thriving Leicester Square and continue
to Piccadilly.

For seediness, walk through Soho (north of Shaftesbury
Avenue) up to Oxford Street. From Piccadilly or Oxford
Circus you can taxi, bus, or tube home. If this is your first
night in Europe, all this activity will keep you up and
then help you sleep.

London Tours
▲▲Original London Sightseeing Tour—This 90-
minute "stay on the bus and enjoy a light once-over of
all the most famous sights with a great commentary"
double-decker tour provides a stressless way to get your
bearings and at least see the famous biggies. (£9, £8 if
you pre-purchase at tourist information offices, daily
departures from 9:45 a.m. until early evening from

Marble Arch, Piccadilly Circus, and Victoria Street, 1 block in front of Victoria Station, reservations unnecessary, tel. 828-7395.) Every other bus comes with a live, and worth waiting for, guide. Bring a sweater and extra film, and pick up the wonderful free city map as you board. You can get a £12 "hop on and hop off" ticket, good for a day (or all the next day if purchased after noon). There are several "original" copy-cat tours.

▲▲**Walking Tours**—Several times every day, top-notch local guides lead small groups through specific slices of London's past. While the TI and many hotels have the various flyers, only *Time Out* and *What's On* list all scheduled walks, enabling you to choose according to your schedule and interests. Simply show up at the announced location, pay £4, and enjoy 2 hours of Dickens, the Plague, Shakespeare, Legal London, the Beatles, Jack the Ripper, or whatever is on the agenda. Evenings feature organized pub crawls and ghost walks. "London Walks" is the dominant company (tel. 624-3978).

London Sightseeing Highlights (in a logical geographical order)

After considering nearly all of London's tourist sights, I have pruned them down to just the most important (or fun) for a first visit. You won't be able to see all of these, so don't try. You'll keep coming back to London. After 15 visits myself, I still enjoy a healthy list of excuses to return.

▲▲**Westminster Abbey** is a crowded collection of England's most famous tombs. It reminds me more of a refugee camp waiting outside St. Peter's gates. This English hall of fame is historic, thought-provoking but a bit over-rated (£3, Monday-Friday 9:20 a.m.-4:00 p.m. and Saturday 9:00 a.m.-2:00 p.m. and 4:00-5:00 p.m. On Wednesday from 6:00-7:45 p.m. only, it's free and photos are allowed. "Super tours" (£3, 90-minutes) leave regularly, tel. 222-5152).

▲▲**The Houses of Parliament** (Commons and Lords) are too tempting to terrorists to be opened wide to tourists. But if parliament is in session, you can view debates in either house at times when most of the building is closed. A light atop Big Ben or a flag flying from the highest tower indi-

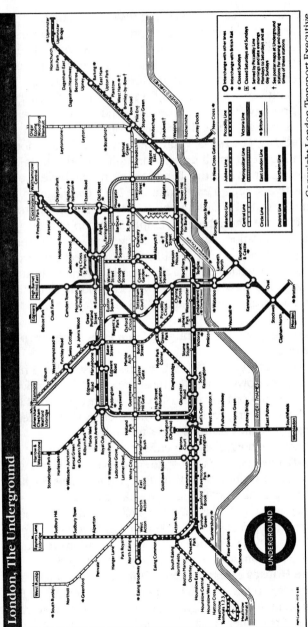

London, The Underground

Copyright London Transport Executive

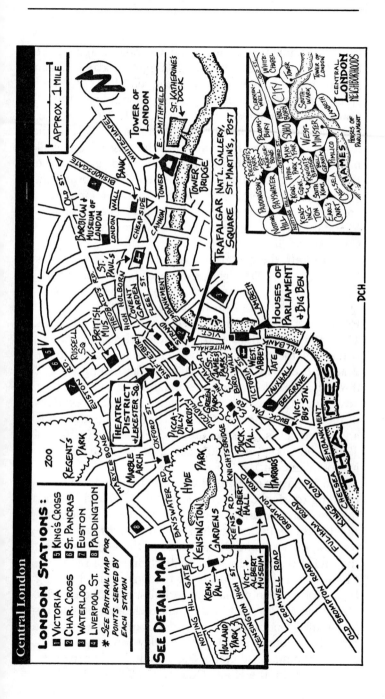

Central London

cates that parliament is in session. (Monday-Thursday 4:15 to 10:00 p.m.—long waits until 6:00 p.m., Friday 9:30 a.m.-3:00 p.m.; use St. Stephens entrance, tel. 219-4272.) The House of Lords has more pageantry, shorter lines, same hours, but less interesting debates (tel. 219-3107). Notice the magnificent hammer-beamed Westminster Hall on the left as you go through security. For the classic view, walk halfway over Westminster Bridge. You won't actually see Big Ben, the 13-ton bell inside the neo-Gothic tower, but you'll hear him. Remember, these old-looking buildings are neo-Gothic—just nineteenth century, reflecting the Victorian move away from neo-Classicism to a more Christian, medieval style.

▲**Whitehall**, the center-of-government boulevard, runs from Big Ben to Trafalgar past lots of important but mostly boring buildings. Stop by the barricade at #10 Downing Street (the British "White House") and the Horse Guards farther up the street (10:00 a.m.-4:00 p.m., 11:00 a.m. inspection, 4:00 p.m. colorful dismounting ceremony, the rest of the day—terrible for camcorders).

▲▲**Cabinet War Rooms**—This is a fascinating walk through the underground headquarters of the British government's fight against the Nazis in the darkest days of the Battle for Britain. Churchill's room, the map room, and so on, are still just as they were in 1945 (£3.60, daily 10:00 a.m.-6:00 p.m., follow signs, on King Charles St., just off Whitehall).

▲**The Banqueting Hall**, England's first Renaissance building (designed by Inigo Jones in 1625) and one of the few London landmarks to survive the 1666 fire, is notable for its Rubens ceiling which, at Charles I's request, drove home the doctrine of the legitimacy of the divine right of kings. In 1649, divine right ignored, Charles I was beheaded on the balcony of this building by a Cromwellian parliament. Admission includes a fine 20-minute audiovisual history, an interesting-only-to-his-tory-buffs 35-minute tape-recorded tour, and a look at a fancy banqueting hall (£2.50, Monday-Saturday 10:00 a.m.-5:00 p.m., aristocratic W.C., immediately across Whitehall from the Horse Guards, tel. 930-4179).

▲▲**Trafalgar Square**—London's central square is a thrilling place to just hang out. There's Lord Nelson's towering column surrounded by giant lions (part of the memorial is made from the melted-down cannons of his victims at Trafalgar), hordes of people, and even more pigeons. (When bombed, resist the impulse to wipe immediately—it'll smear. Wait for it to dry and flake off gently.) The square is the climax of most marches and demonstrations.

▲▲**National Gallery**—Newly renovated, displaying Britain's top collection of European paintings from 1300 to 1900—works by Leonardo, Botticelli, Velazquez, Rembrandt, Turner, van Gogh, and the Impressionists—this is one of Europe's classiest galleries. Don't miss the "Micro Gallery," a computer room even your dad could have fun in. You can study any artist, style, or topic in the museum and even print out a tailor-made tour map. (Free, Monday-Saturday 10:00 a.m.-6:00 p.m., Sunday 2:00-6:00 p.m., on Trafalgar Square. Tube: Charing Cross or Leicester Square, free 1-hour tours weekdays at 11:30 and 2:30, Saturdays at 2:00 and 3:30, tel. 839-3321). The National Portrait Gallery is just around the corner and as exciting as somebody else's yearbook (free, tel. 306-0055).

▲▲**Piccadilly**—London's touristy "Town Square" is surrounded by fascinating streets and swimming with youth on the rampage. Nearby Shaftesbury Avenue and Leicester Square teem with fun-seekers, theaters, Chinese restaurants, and street singers. Soho, to the north, isn't as sleazy as it used to be, but it's still worth a gawk. The shiny new Trocadero Center (between Coventry and Shaftesbury, just off Piccadilly) has the Guinness World Records Exhibit. Next door, the new Rock Circus offers a very commercial but serious history of rock music with Madame Tussaud wax stars. It's an entertaining hour under radio earphones for rock 'n' roll romantics (£6.50, plenty of photo ops, open late).

▲**Covent Gardens** is a boutique-ish people-watcher's delight with cigarette-eaters, Punch 'n' Judy acts, food that's good for you (but not for your wallet), trendy crafts, whiffs of pot, and two-tone (neither natural) hair. For the best lunch deals, walk a block or two away from the eye of this touristic tornado. It's hard to go wrong in a little tea-and-sandwich deli.

▲▲▲**British Museum**—The greatest chronicle of our civilization anywhere, visiting this immense museum is like hiking through Encyclopedia Britannica National Park. After an overview ramble, cover just two or three sections of your choice more thoroughly. The Egyptian, Mesopotamian, Greek (Parthenon), and Manuscripts (Magna Carta, Bibles, Beethoven, and the Beatles) sections are a few of my favorites. (Free, Monday-Saturday 10:00 a.m.-5:00 p.m., Sunday 2:30-6:00 p.m., least crowded weekday mornings, tube: Tottenham Court Road, tel. 323-8299.)

▲**Buckingham Palace**—In order to pay for the restoration of fire-damaged Windsor Palace, the royal family is opening up their lavish "home" to the public for the next five summers. (£8, summer only, daily 9:30 a.m.-5:30 p.m., limited to 8,000 a day, come early to get an appointed visit time, tel. 930-5526, if the queen's not home, leave a message.) If the flag is flying, the queen is home.

▲**Changing of the Guard at Buckingham Palace**— Overrated but almost required. The changing of the guard (most days in summer at 11:30 a.m., every other day September-March) is a mob scene. Join the mob at the back side of the palace (the front faces a huge and very private park). The pageantry and parading are colorful and even stirring, but the actual changing of the guard is a non-event. It is interesting to see nearly every tourist in London gathered in one place at the same time. Hop in a big black taxi and say, "To Buckingham Palace, please." For all the color with none of the crowds, see the Inspection of the Guard Ceremony at 11:00 a.m. in front of the Wellington Barracks, east of the Palace on Birdcage Walk. Afterwards, stroll through nearby St. James Park.

▲**Hyde Park**—London's "Central Park" has more than 600 acres of lush greenery, a huge manmade lake, a royal palace, and the ornate neo-Gothic Albert Memorial across from the Royal Albert Hall. On Sunday early afternoons, check out Speaker's Corner (tube: Marble Arch). This is soapbox oratory at its best. "The grass roots of democracy" actually is a holdover from when the gallows stood here and the criminal was allowed to say just about anything he wanted to before he swung. I dare you to raise your voice and gather a crowd—it's easy to do.

▲▲**The City of London**—When Londoners say "the City," they mean the one-square-mile business, banking, and journalism center that 2,000 years ago was Roman Londinium. The outline of the Roman city walls can still be seen in the arc of roads from Blackfriars Bridge to Tower Bridge. Within the City are 24 churches designed by Christopher Wren. It's a fascinating district to wander, but since nobody actually lives there, avoid Saturday and Sunday when it's quiet and empty.

Also worth a look is the Central Criminal Courts, known as "Old Bailey." An hour in the visitors' gallery is always interesting (at Old Bailey and Newgate St., Monday-Friday 10:00 a.m.-1:00 p.m. and 2:00-4:00 p.m., quiet in August, tel. 248-3277, no cameras, bags, or cloak room).

▲▲**St. Paul's Cathedral**—Wren's most famous church is the great St. Paul's, its elaborate interior capped by a 365-foot dome. St. Paul's was Britain's World War II symbol of resistance, as Nazi bombs failed to blow it up. (There's a memorial chapel to the heroic firefighters who kept watch over it with hoses cocked.) The crypt (free with admission) is a world of historic bones and memorials, including Admiral Nelson's tomb. It also has interesting Cathedral models and a worthwhile 15-minute audiovisual story of the church (constant, free). It was the wedding church of Prince Charles and Lady Di. Climb the dome for a great city view and some fun in the whispering gallery. Talk—discreetly—into the wall and your partner on the far side can hear you. (£2.50 entry, free on Sunday but restricted viewing due to services, open daily 9:30-4:30, £2.50 to climb the dome, allow an hour to go up and down—good exercise, 90-minute £3 cathedral and crypt tours at 11:00, 11:30, 1:30 and 2:00, tube: St. Paul's.)

The **Sir Christopher Wren Pub** (not restaurant) serves good, inexpensive lunches in fun surroundings, just north of the church on Paternoster Square, 11:30 a.m.-3:00 p.m., Monday-Friday.

▲**Museum of London** offers a guided walk through
London history—from pre-Roman times to the Blitz (£3,
10:00 a.m.-6:00 p.m., Sunday 2:00-6:00 p.m., tube:
Barbican or St. Paul's).

▲▲▲**Tower of London**—You'll find more bloody history per square inch here than anywhere in Britain.
Don't miss the entertaining 50-minute Beefeater tour
(free, leaving regularly from inside the gate, last one at
3:30 p.m.) of this historic fortress, palace, prison, and
host to more than 3 million visitors a year. Britain's best
armory and most lovely Norman chapel are in the White
Tower. The crown jewels are the best on earth—and
consequently have long midday lines for viewing in July
and August. To avoid the crowds, arrive at 9:00 a.m. and
go straight to the jewels, doing the tour and tower later.
(£6.70, tower hours: Monday-Saturday 9:00 a.m.-6:00
p.m., last entry 5:00 p.m., Sunday 10:00 a.m.-6:00 p.m.
The long, but fast-moving, line is worst on Sundays.
Tube: Tower Hill. Tel. 709-0765.) Visitors are welcome
on the grounds to worship in the Royal Chapel on
Sunday (9:15 a.m. communion, 11:00 a.m. service with
fine choral music, free).

Sights Next to the Tower:
The best remaining bit of London's Roman Wall is just
north of the tower (at the Tower Hill tube station).

The Tower Hill Pageant, a 15-minute high-tech historical amusement ride takes you through twenty centuries
of London history, followed by a small but fine exhibition of Roman and Saxon artifacts uncovered during the
recent riverside development. It's worthwhile for rich
kids with time to kill (£5, daily 9:30 a.m.-5:30 p.m., until
4:30 off-season, across the street from the Tower turnstile, tel. 709-0081).

Freshly painted and restored, Tower Bridge celebrates
its 100th birthday with an 1894-1994 history exhibit
(£3.50, daily from 10:00 a.m., tel. 378-1928). Good view,
marginal value.

St. Katherine Yacht Harbor, chic and newly renovated,
just east of the Tower Bridge, has mod shops and the
classic old Dickens Inn, fun for a drink or pub lunch.

▲▲**Cruise the Thames**—Boat tours with an entertaining commentary sail regularly between Westminster Bridge and the Tower (£3, 10:20 a.m.-5:00 p.m., 30 minutes, three tours hourly, tel. 930-4097). Leaving from Westminster pier, similar boats also go to Greenwich (£5 round-trip, two hourly) and Kew Gardens (£7 round-trip, tel. 930-4721).

▲▲**Greenwich**—Salty sightseers should make time for England's maritime capital, Greenwich. You can crawl through the *Cutty Sark* (clipper-ship queen of the seas in her day), marvel at the little Gipsy Moth IV (the 53-foot sailboat Sir Francis Chichester used for his solo voyage around the world in 1967), straddle the zero meridian and set your wristwatch to Greenwich mean time at the Old Royal Observatory, and relive four centuries of Brittania-rules-the-waves history by visiting the National Maritime Museum (10:00 a.m.-6:00 p.m., Sundays noon-6:00 p.m., off-season until 5:00 p.m., tel. 081/858-4422). Getting there is either a snap (tube to Island Gardens in zone two, free with tube pass, then walk under pedestrian Thames tunnel) or a joy (cruise down the Thames from central London).

▲▲**Tate Gallery**—One of Europe's great houses of art, the Tate specializes in British painting (fourteenth century through contemporary), pre-Raphaelites, Impressionism and modern art (Matisse, van Gogh, Monet, Picasso). Learn about the mystical watercolorist Blake and the romantic nature-worship art of Turner (free, Monday-Saturday 10:00 a.m.-6:00 p.m., Sunday 2:00-6:00 p.m., tube: Pimlico, excellent free tours daily, call for schedule, tel. 821-1313).

▲**Victoria and Albert Museums**—A gangly but surprisingly interesting collection of costumes, armor, furniture, decorative arts, and much more. (£3.50 donation requested, 10:00 a.m.-6:00 p.m., Sunday 2:30-6:00 p.m., closed Friday, tube: So. Kensington.)

▲▲**Imperial War Museum**—This impressive museum covers the wars of this century from heavy weaponry to love notes and Vargas Girls to Monty's Africa campaign tank to Schwartzkopf's Desert Storm uniform (a real high-

light for many). You can trace the development of the
machine gun, watch footage of the first tank battles, hold
your breath through the gruesome WWI trench experience, and buy WWII-era toys in the fun museum shop.
The museum doesn't glorify war, it shines a light on the
powerful human side of one of mankind's most persistent
traits. (£3.70, daily 10:00 a.m.-6:00 p.m., free after 4:30
p.m., 90 minutes is enough time for most visitors, tube:
Lambeth North.)

▲▲Museum of the Moving Image: This high-tech, inter-
active, hands-on museum traces the story of moving
images from a caveman's flickering fire to modern TV.
There's great footage of the earliest movies and TV shows.
Turn-of-the-century-clad staff speak as if silent films are
the latest marvel. You can make your own animated cartoon. Don't miss the speedy fifty-year montage of magic
MGM moments. (£3.75, daily 10:00 a.m.-6:00 p.m., tube:
Embankment, then walk across the Thames pedestrian
bridge.)

Honorable Mention: The Thames Barrier, the world's
largest movable flood barrier, welcomes visitors with an
informative and entertaining exhibition (by tube or boat,
£2.25, daily 10:30 a.m.-5:00 p.m., tel. 081/854-1373). At
the Geffrye Decorative Arts Museum, you can walk
through British front rooms from 1600 to 1960 (tel. 739-
9893). Architects love the quirky Sir John Soane's Museum
(free). For a fine park and a palatial greenhouse jungle to
swing through, take the tube or the boat to Kew Gardens
(£3, daily from 9:30 a.m., tel. 081/940-1171).

Shopping
▲Harrods—This is one of the few stores in the world
that manages to be both big and classy. Wonderful displays, elegant high teas, fingernail-ripping riots during the
July sales. Harrods has everything from elephants to
toothbrushes. Need some peanut butter? The food halls
are sights to savor (with reasonable cafeterias). For royal
window-shopping, cruise nearby King's Road in Chelsea.
Most stores close around 6:00 p.m., but stay open until
8:00 p.m. on Thursdays.

Street Markets—If you like garage sales and people-watching, hit a London street market. The tourist office has a complete, up-to-date list. Some of the best are:
Berwick Street (Monday-Saturday 9:00 a.m.-5:00 p.m., produce, tube: Piccadilly), **Jubilee Market** (daily 9:00 a.m.-5:00 p.m., antiques and bric-a-brac on Monday, general miscellany Tuesday-Friday, crafts Saturday-Sunday, tube: Covent Garden), **Kensington Market** (Monday-Saturday 10:00 a.m.-6:00 p.m., a collection of shops with modern and far-out clothing, tube: High Street Kensington), **Petticoat Lane** (Sunday 9:00 a.m.-1:30 p.m., the largest, specializing in general junk, on Middlesex St., tube: Liverpool St.), **Portobello Road** (Saturday 6:00 a.m.-5:00 p.m., flea market, near recommended B&Bs, tube: Notting Hill Gate), and **Camden Market** (Saturday and Sunday 9:00 a.m.-5:00 p.m., a big trendy flea market, tube: Camden Town), and Camden Passage (Wednesday and Saturday 8:30 a.m.-3:00 p.m., lots of expensive antiques on Islington High St., tube: Angel). Warning: street markets attract two kinds of people—tourists and pickpockets.

Famous Auction?—London's famous auctioneers welcome the curious public. For schedules (most weekdays, closed mid-summer), telephone Sotheby's (493-8080, tube: Oxford Circus) or Christie's (839-9060, tube: Green Park).

Entertainment and Theater

London bubbles with top-notch entertainment seven nights a week. The key to maximizing your entertainment pleasure is to take advantage of *Time Out* or *What's On* magazines, available at most newsstands. You'll choose from classical, jazz, rock, and far-out music, Gilbert and Sullivan, dance, comedy, Bahai meetings, poetry readings, spectator sports, film, and theater.

I focus on theater. London's theater rivals Broadway's in quality and beats it in price. Choose from the Royal Shakespeare Company, top musicals, comedy, thrillers, sex farces, and more. Performances are nightly except Sunday, usually with one matinee a week. Matinees (listed in a box in *What's On*) are cheaper and rarely sold out. Tickets range from about £8 to £25.

Most theaters, marked on tourist maps, are in the Piccadilly-Trafalgar area. Box offices, hotels, and TIs have a very handy "Theater Guide" brochure listing everything in town.

The best and cheapest way to book a ticket is simply to call the theater box office directly, ask about seats and dates available, and book by credit card. You can call from the U.S.A. as easily as from England (photocopy your hometown library's London newspaper theater section). Pick up your ticket 15 minutes before the show.

Getting a ticket through a ticket agency (at most tourist offices or scattered throughout London) is quick and easy, but prices are inflated by a standard 20 to 25 percent booking fee. Ticket agencies are scalpers with an address. Agencies are worthwhile only if a show you've got to see is sold out at the box office. Various ticket agencies scarf up hot tickets, planning to make a killing after the show is otherwise sold out. U.S.A. booking agencies get their tickets from another agency, adding to your expense by involving yet another middleman.

Cheap theater tricks: Most theaters offer cheap returned tickets, standing room, matinee, and senior or student stand-by deals. Picking up a late return can get you a great seat at a cheap seat price. Standing room costs only a few pounds. If a show is "sold out," there's usually a way to get a seat. Call and ask how. The famous "half-price booth" in Leicester (pronounced "Lester") Square sells cheap tickets to shows on the push list the day of the show only (2:30-6:30 p.m., Monday-Saturday). I usually buy the second-cheapest tickets directly from the theater box office. Many theaters are so small that there's hardly a bad seat. "Scooting up" later on is less than a capital offense.

Royal Shakespeare Company: If you'll ever enjoy Shakespeare, it'll be here. (But lo, I've tried and failed.) The RSC splits its 12-play April-through-January season between the Royal Shakespeare Theatre in Stratford (tel. 0789/295623; recorded information tel. 0789/269191) and the Barbican Centre (open until 11:00 p.m. daily; credit-card booking; tel. 071/638-8891, tel. recorded information: 071/628-2295). Tickets range in price from £8 to £22. For a complete schedule, write to the Royal Shakespeare Theatre, Stratford-upon-Avon, Warwickshire, CV37 6BB, or call 0789/205301. Shakespeare fans stay tuned for the opening of the reconstructed Globe Theater (1995?) which will be doing Shakespeare as it was done in his day.

Music: For a fun classical event, attend a "Prom Concert." This is an annual music festival with almost nightly concerts in the Royal Albert Hall from July through September at give-a-peasant-some-culture prices (£3 standing-room spots sold at the door, tel. 589-8212). Look into the free lunchtime concerts popular in churches (listed at TI, especially Wren's St. Brides' Church, tel. 353-1301, and St. Martin-In-The-Fields, tel. 930-1862).

The ultimate round of beer: The London tube's Circle Line makes 21 stops during each orbit. There just happens to be a pub near the entry of each of these tube stops. A popular game is to race around trying to drink a pint (or a half-pint) at each of the 21 bars between the "old" pub hours (5:30 to 11:00 p.m.). Twenty-one pints is about 2 gallons of beer. Locals prefer starting at the Farrington stop. A few of the pubs are tough to find—ask at the nearest newsstand for directions.

Itinerary Options—Day Trips from London
London is surrounded by exciting, easy day-trip destinations. Several tour companies take London-based travelers out and back every day (call Evan Evans at 930-2377 or National Express at 730-0202 for ideas). When you consider that an all-day guided bus tour from London to Stonehenge and Bath and back costs the same as a one-way London-Bath train ticket (£25), day-tours are worth pondering.

The British rail system uses London as a hub and normally offers round-trip fares (after 9:30 a.m.) that cost the same as one-way fares. See BritRail's handy "Day Trips from London" booklet. For the serious day-tripper, *Daytrips in Britain by Rail, Bus or Car from London and*

Edinburgh is a great guidebook, including 60 one-day adventures (Earl Steinbicker, Hastings House).

London uses a different train station for each destination region. For schedule information, call the appropriate station: King's Cross (northeast England, Scotland), 278-2477; Paddington (west and southwest England, south Wales), 262-6767; most others, 928-5100.

Accommodations in London (£1 = about $1.50, tel. code: 071)

London has hundreds of reasonable hotels but few great deals. There's no need, however, to spend a fortune or stay in a dangerous, depressing dump. Plan on spending about £45 (about $70) for a basic, clean, decent double in a usually cramped, cracked-plaster building with an English (as opposed to continental) breakfast. In the cheaper places, service is minimal. (Hang up your towel to dry and reuse). Unless otherwise noted, assume that the price includes a big English breakfast in a breakfast room, and that they'll hold a room with a phone call and a credit card number. If you're on a tight budget traveling off-season (September to June), you'll save a few pounds if you arrive late without a reservation; call and ask for a deal.

I reserve my London room in advance with a phone call direct from the States (dial 011/44/71/London phone number). Assure the manager you'll arrive before 4:00 p.m. and leave your credit card number as security. If you must send a deposit, send a signed $100 traveler's check. (Leave the "pay to" line blank and include a note explaining that you'll be happy to pay cash upon arrival, so they can avoid bank charges, if they'll just hold your check until you get there.)

Victoria Station Area

The streets behind Victoria Station teem with budget B&Bs. It's a safe, surprisingly tidy and decent area without a hint of the trashy touristy glitz of the streets in front of the station. The first three listings are on Ebury street, between the train and coach stations, proudly part of Bel-

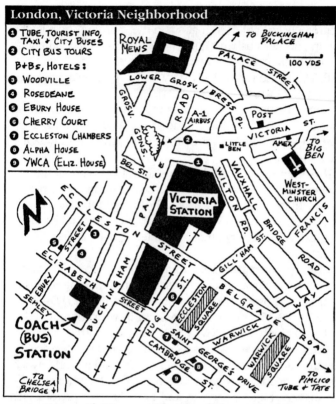

London, Victoria Neighborhood

❶ TUBE, TOURIST INFO, TAXI + CITY BUSES
❷ CITY BUS TOURS

B+Bs, HOTELS:

❸ WOODVILLE
❹ ROSEDEANE
❺ EBURY HOUSE
❻ CHERRY COURT
❼ ECCLESTON CHAMBERS
❽ ALPHA HOUSE
❾ YWCA (ELIZ. HOUSE)

gravia. Even with Margaret Thatcher living around the corner (you'll see the policeman standing outside of #73 Chester Square), this is a classy and peaceful place to call home in London. Neighboring Elizabeth Street is the neighborhood center for shops and eateries (#23 for take-out or eat-in fish and chips). The Duke of Wellington pub (63 Eaton Terrace, meals 6:00-10:30 p.m., not Sunday) is good for dinner. While Ebury has traffic, the last two listings (on Warwick Way), are the only ones with a traffic noise problem. All are within a 5-minute walk of the Victoria tube and train station.

Woodville House is an oasis of small-town warmth and hospitality in downtown London. As in most budget hotels, the quarters are tight, but you'll get a small garden, home-made müesli, color-coordinated decor, orthopedic beds, lots of travel tips, endless tea, coffee, and friendly chat (especially about the local rich and famous) from the "extremely sociable, even at six in the morning" host Rachel Joplin and her husband Ian. (S-£35, D-£50, bunky family deals for three, four, or five in a room, showers down the hall, TVs in the room; 107 Ebury Street, Belgravia, SW1W 9QU, tel. 730-1048, fax 730-2574).

Ebury House is another maximum homey place enthusiastically run by friendly Mr. and Mrs. Davies (S-£40, D-£50, T-£66, Q-£75, TVs in rooms; 102 Ebury Street, SW1W 9QD, tel. 730-1350).

Rosedene Hotel, on the same fine street without the homey flair, is not as cramped as others in this price range. Its breakfast room doubles as a TV lounge (absentee owners, S-£26, D-£38, T-£50, Q-£64, only a continental breakfast, CC-V; 119 Ebury Street, SW1, tel. 730-4872, fax 224-6902).

Cherry Court Hotel is a minimal little place, plain and cramped but very close to the station and offering rooms at near-youth-hostel prices on a quiet street (SB-£25, D-£28, DB-£32, TB-35, continental breakfast in your room, CC-VMA; 23 Hugh Street, SW1V 1QJ, tel. 828-2840).

Eccleston Chambers is a big "Hotel and Conference Centre" facing a stately square, 3 blocks and a world away from Victoria Station. All rooms have TVs, telephones, coffee makers, bath or shower, and even "trouser presses." It's quiet, spacious, and has an elevator (SB-from £35, DB-from £45, TB-from £50, QB-from £55, CC-VM; 30 Eccleston Square, SW1V 2NZ, tel. 828-7924 and 828-7925, fax 828-7924).

Alfa Hotel has thirty small rooms and narrow hallways, but offers more homey touches per square inch than any other. The place has a Pompeiien feel with tiny statues, fluted headboards, antique furniture carefully chosen to fill tiny corners, and a small walled garden. All rooms have TVs, telephones, a shower or bath, and coffee makers (SB-£39, DB-from £49, TB-£68, QB-£80, "deluxe" rooms are £6 extra, CC-VMA; 78-82 Warwick Way, Victoria, SW1, tel. 828-8603, fax 976-6536).

Elizabeth House YWCA offers people of any sex inexpensive beds in a big, friendly, musty place with narrow yellow halls, stark rooms, and bad news carpets (S-£20, D-

£40, DB-£45, shared T and Q-£15 per bed, with a buffet continental breakfast, request a quiet room off the street; 118 Warwick Way, SW1V 1SD, tel. 630-0741).

"South Kensington," he said, loosening his cummerbund.

For a chance to live on a quiet street so classy it doesn't allow hotel signs, surrounded by trendy shops and colorful eateries, 350 yards from the handy "South Kensington" tube station (on the Circle Line, direct connection to Heathrow, two stops from Victoria Station), call South Kensington home in London. Shoppers will enjoy the location, a short walk from Harrods and the designer shops of King's Road and Chelsea. You'll find plenty of ethnic and colorful budget eateries around the corner on Brompton Road. This has got to be the ultimate fairy-tale London home away from home. Of course, you'll pay for it. But these places are a fine value.

Five Sumner Place Hotel is informal but professional and "highly commended." You'll talk softly but not feel like you have to dress up as you wander, with your free daily newspaper, under the chandeliers out to the Victorian-style conservatory, a greenhouse dressed in blue, for breakfast. Each room is tastefully decorated with traditional period furnishings in a 150-year-old building (SB-£65, DB-£90, TB-£105, all with TV and telephone, elevator, CC-VMA, 5 Sumner Place, South Kensington, SW7 3EE, tel. 584-7586, fax 823-9962, if enough of you sleep here, maybe they'll give me a free room).

The Prince Hotel, right next door, is relatively dumpy (but still nice). It also has an elegant, glass-covered conservatory, period decor throughout, and TVs and telephones in each of its twenty rooms. Its cheaper rooms ("without facilities," meaning with a shower but the toilet's down the hall) are an especially good value (SB-£46, SBWC-£59, DB-£59, DBWC-£72, QBWC-£106; 6 Sumner Place, SW7 3AB, CC-VMA, tel. 589-6488, fax 581-0824).

Aster House Hotel also offers you a chance to be elegant in London without going broke. The hotel's brochure reminds guests when they're going out to L'Orangerie (Victorian greenhouse) for breakfast, "To be considerate of your table companions, your neighbors and your hosts, we hope to welcome you in elegant attire, even if relaxed." Each room has a TV, telephone, fridge and separate bathroom. Their third-floor rooms (no elevator) are the best deal. (SB-£52, DB on 3rd fl.-£68, DB-from £78, CC-VM, CC deposits non-refundable if you cancel with less than two weeks notice; 3 Sumner Place, SW7 3EE, tel. 581-5888, fax 584-4925).

Notting Hill Gate Area

When in London, I live in Notting Hill Gate. It's residential, with quick and easy bus or tube access to downtown, on the A2 Airbus line from Heathrow (second stop from airport, after Kensington Hilton), relatively safe (except for the dangerous, riot-plagued Notting Hill Carnival, the last weekend of August), and for London, very "homely." Notting Hill Gate has a late-hours supermarket, self-serve launderette, great theater, and lots of fun budget eateries (see Food below). Here are a few of my favorite hotels. All are near the Holland Park or Notting Hill Gate tube station. (Notting Hill Gate is in the central zone and on the Circle Line, handier and 40p cheaper from anywhere than the Holland Park station.)

Vicarage Private Hotel is understandably popular. Family-run and elegantly British in a quiet, classy neighborhood, it has 19 rooms furnished with taste and quality. Martin, Mandy, and Mark maintain a homey and caring atmosphere. Lots of stairs, a TV lounge, TVs in most rooms, facilities on each floor. Reserve long in advance with a one-night deposit. (S-£30, D-£52, T-£60, Q-£70, a 6-minute walk from the Notting Hill Gate and High Street Kensington tube stations near Kensington Palace at 10 Vicarage Gate, Kensington, W8 4AG, tel. 229-4030).

Abbey House Hotel is similar in almost every way to its neighbor, the Vicarage Private Hotel. It's a few pounds more expensive, with no lounge and a bit less cozy (S-£30, D-£52, T-£62, Q-£72, Quint-£82; 11 Vicarage Gate, Kensington, W8, tel. 727-2594).

London, Holland Park Neighborhood

Hotel Ravna Gora—Formerly Mr. Holland's mansion, now it's a large Yugoslavian-run B&B, eccentric and well-worn but comfortable, spacious, and handy for the price. Manda and Rijko take good care of their guests with a royal TV room and a good (but no OJ) English breakfast. Plain bright rooms, grand old creaky spiral staircase, easy parking, avoid the noisy street-front rooms (S-£27, D-£44, DB-£54, T-£51, TB-£63, Q-£64, QB-£76; 50 yards from Holland Park tube station, 29 Holland Park Ave., W11, tel. 727-7725, fax 221-4282).

Dean Court Hotel—This wild and crazy Aussie hangout offers young travelers good basic facilities (£11 beds in 3- to 5-bedded rooms, D-£32, Twins-£35; 100 yards from Bayswater Tube, 57 Inverness Terrace, W2, reservations with deposit only unless one night before, tel. 229-2961, fax 727-1190).

Holland Park Hotel—Professional and "hotelesque", but a fine value with a remarkably personal touch. Royal lounge, cheery staff, sleepy garden, TVs in rooms, buffet continental breakfast, quiet, on a pleasant woodsy street, easy credit-card reservations (S-£38, SB-£47, D-£47, DB-£64, extra beds £12, CC-VMA; 6 Ladbrook Terrace, W11 3PG, tel. 792-0216, fax 727-8166).

Westend Hotel is comfortable and convenient but strict and not terribly flavorful (DB-£70, £60 in the annex, elevator, all rooms with TV, telephone, hairdryers, coffee makers, and so on, CC-VMA, reserve with a deposit; 154 Bayswater Road, W2 4HP, tel. 229-9191, fax 727-1054).

Methodist International House—This Christian residence, filled mostly with Asian and African students, is great if you want a truly worldwide dorm experience at a price that will bolster your faith. Each smoke-free room is studious with a desk and reading lamp. The atmosphere is friendly, safe and controlled but well-worn with a silent study room, reading lounge, TV lounge, game room, and laundry facilities (£16 beds in shared doubles or triples, S-£20, D-£34, T-£48, includes breakfast and a cafeteria dinner—no typo; near Bayswater tube and a block from Queensway tube on a quiet street, 2 Inverness Terrace, W2 3HY, tel. 229-5101.)

Norwegian YWCA (Norsk K.F.U.K.)—For women under 25 only (and men with Norwegian passports), this is an incredible value—smoke-free, Norwegian atmosphere, on quiet stately street, piano lounge, TV room, study, all rooms with private shower. They have mostly quads, so those willing to share with strangers are most likely to get a place. (June-August: SB-£23, bed in shared double-£23, shared quad-£17, with breakfast. September-May: prices go down and include breakfast and dinner. Monthly rates-£10 a day in shared quad with breakfast and dinner. 52 Holland Park, W11 3R5, tel. 727-9897). I wonder which is easier—getting a sex change or a Norwegian passport?

Holland Park Independent Hostel (S-£15, D-£26, T-£36, bed in small unisex dorm-£10, no breakfast; 41 Holland Park, tel. 229-4238) has spacious ramshackle rooms, a TV lounge, no lockers, member's kitchen and bugs. On an aristocratic quiet street, it's a lovely alternative to the bushes.

Accommodations in London's Bloomsbury District

These places are between the British Museum and King's Cross Station, all within 3 blocks of the Russell Square tube station. For the first three, Leigh Street is a handy place to find fish and chips, Indian, Chinese or pub grub. The last two are on an elegant and quiet street 2 blocks from the British Museum.

Cambria House, an amazing value, is run by the Salvation Army. (Relax, this is a good thing when it comes to cheap big-city hotels.) This smoke-free old building with a narrow maze of halls is all newly painted (cheap hotel-yellow) and super clean—if institutional. The rooms are spacious and perfectly good. There are ample showers and toilets on each floor and a TV lounge (S-£20, D-£31, DB-£40, T-£31, CC-VM; north of Russell Square at 37 Hunter Street, WC1N 1BJ, tel. 837-1654, fax 837-1229).

Harlingford Hotel is the popular queen (and most expensive) of a line of budget hotels along a green crescent (S-£47, only two D-£48, DB-£60, TB-£70, QB-£80, CC-VM; 61 Cartwright Gardens, WC1H 9EL, tel. 387-1551, fax 387-4616).

Jenkins Hotel, recommended mainly because that's my wife's maiden name, is family-run and comfortable, but a bit cramped in a small building with 12 rooms and lots of narrow stairs (S-£33, D-£56, telephone, fridge and TV in each room, CC-VM; 45 Cartwright Gardens, WC1H 9EH, tel. 387-2067, fax 383-3139).

Repton Hotel is the cheapest and most run-down of several hotels on an elegant Georgian Terrace 2 minutes' walk from the British Museum. Prices may be soft, and with luck during slow times, you may get a dorm to yourself, in which case it's a great value. (S-£30, D-£44, DB-£56, 6-bed dorms-£12 per person, with a continental breakfast, TV in each room; 31 Bedford Place, WC1B 5JH, tel. 436-4922, tel. and fax 636-7045). The Thanet (at #8 across the street, tel. 636-2869) is much nicer, but more expensive.

Central University of Iowa Hostel rents to non-Iowans from early May through late August. It's clean, basic, and reminiscent of elegance with plenty of facilities (study room, TV lounge, washer and dryer). (D-£32, beds in 3- to

5-bed rooms-£16, with continental breakfast; 7 Bedford Place, WC1B 5JA, tel. 580-1121).

Accommodations in Other Areas

Mary Ward's Guest House—Sleepable but very simple on a quiet street in a rough-and-tumble neighborhood south of Victoria near Clapham Common, this beats the hostels. Friendly Mary Ward (Edith Bunker's English aunt) has been renting her five super-cheap rooms to budget travelers for 25 years. (S-£10, D-£20 with English breakfast, 98 Hambalt Rd., Clapham Common, London, tel. 081/673-1077, 15 minutes by tube to Clapham Common and a 12-minute walk— exit left down Chapham South Road, left on Elms, right on Abbeville Road, left on Hambalt.)

Lynwood Guest House—Out of London (30 minutes by train) near Gatwick Airport (10 minutes by train), this place offers a cozy, friendly alternative to big-city lodging in Redhill, a normal work-a-day English town. Easy parking, a 5-minute walk from train station, owner Shanta may pick you up, genuinely caring and gracious (SB-£24, DB-£36, TB-£50, QB-£56; 50 London Rd., Redhill, Surrey RH1 1LN, tel. 0737/766894).

The Crutchfield Inn B&B—(DB-£45, 2 miles from Gatwick airport, 30 minutes by train from London, at Hookwood, Surrey, RH6OHT, tel. 0293/863110, fax 863233), offers 3 comfortable rooms in a 500-year-old renovated farmhouse. Mrs. Blok includes a ride to and from the airport.

Oxford Street Youth Hostel (£17 beds with sheets, D-£34, no breakfast, open 24 hours, lockers, mean elevator; 14-18 Noel St., London W1, tube: Oxford Street, tel. 071/734-1618), downtown, new, with spartan and modern 2- and 4-bed rooms, is worth it only if you want to sleep with the hosteling gang and be right downtown.

Food
If you want to dine (as opposed to eat), check out the extensive listings in *What's On*. The thought of a £20 meal generally ruins my appetite, so my London dining is limited mostly to unremarkable, but inexpensive, alternatives.

Your £5 budget choices are pub grub, a café, fish and chips, pizza, ethnic, or picnic.

Pub grub is the most atmospheric budget option. Many of London's 7,000 pubs serve fresh, tasty buffets under ancient timbers with hearty lunches and dinners priced around £5. Ethnic restaurants from all over the world more than make up for the basically lackluster English cuisine. Eating Indian or Chinese is "going local" in London. It's also going cheap (cheaper if you take out). Pizza places all over town offer £3.50 all-you-can-stomach buffets. Of course, picnicking is the fastest and cheapest way to go. There are plenty of good grocery stores and sandwich shops, fine park benches, and polite pigeons in Britain's most expensive city.

If nothing here sounds tasty, London's Restaurant Switchboard (tel. 444-0044, Monday-Saturday until 8:00 p.m.) can give you lots of thoughts for food.

Eating near Trafalgar Square: For a meal on a monk's budget in an ancient crypt sitting on somebody's tomb, climb down into the **St.-Martin-in-the-Fields** Restaurant (10:00-8:00, Sunday 12:00-6:00, £5-£7 cafeteria plates, cheaper sandwich bar, profits go to the church; underneath St.-Martin-in-the-Fields on Trafalgar Square, tel. 839-4342). Down Whitehall (towards Big Ben), a block from Trafalgar Square, you'll find the atmospheric Clarence Pub (decent grub) and several cheaper cafeterias and pizza joints. For a classy lunch, treat your palate to the pricier **Brasserie** (first floor, Sainsbury Wing of the National Gallery).

Eating near Piccadilly: Wren at St. James Church coffeehouse (8:00 a.m.-7:00 p.m., Sunday 10:00 a.m.-4:00 p.m., not exclusively vegetarian, 2 minutes off Piccadilly, at 35 Jermyn St., tel. 437-9419) is wonderfully green and in a pleasant garden next to one of Wren's best churches (peek in). **Stockpot** is famous and rightly popular for its tasty budget meals (even cheaper before 5:00 p.m., 8:00 a.m. to 11:30 p.m., Sunday noon-10:30 p.m., 40 Panton St., off Haymarket near Piccadilly). **Deep Pan Pizza** has a £3.50 buffet (daily 11:30 a.m. to 11:30 p.m., 18 Lower Regent Street).

The palatial **Criterion Restaurant** (tel. 925-0909), serving
a two-course dinner for £10 under gilded tiles and chandeliers, is 20 yards and a world away from the punk junk of
Piccadilly Circus. The **Carvery** serves a £15 all-you-can-
eat meaty buffet with plenty of vegetables and a salad
bar, Yorkshire and bread pudding, dessert and coffee
included—a carnivore's delight with concessions to vegetar-
ians. Puffy-hatted carvers help you slice. (Regent Palace
Hotel on Glasshouse St., a cigarette-butt toss from Piccadilly
Circus, noon-2:30 p.m. and 5:15-9:00 p.m., Sunday 12:30-
2:30 p.m. and 6:00-9:00 p.m.).

**Restaurants near Recommended Notting Hill Gate
B&Bs:** Try **Costas** for Greek food or eat-in or take-out fish
and chips (£5 meals, closed Sunday, near the Coronet Theatre at Hillgate Street #18). Next door, the **Hillgate Pub**
has good food and famous hot saltbeef sandwiches
(indoor/outdoor, closed Sunday). The not-too-spicy **Mod-
hubon** Indian restaurant is worth the moderate splurge
(cheap lunch specials, 29 Pembridge Road, tel. 727-3399).
There's a cheap Chinese take-out next door (19 Pembridge
Road, 5:30 p.m. to midnight nightly). The **Arc** on Kensington Palace Gardens Street is small, popular and worth the
moderate splurge (£15 meals, go early or call ahead, 6:30-
11:15 p.m. nightly, tel. 229-4024). **"CAPS"** restaurant (64
Pembridge Road, open 6:00 to 11:15 p.m., tel. 229-5177)
serves tasty £10 meals. On Kensington Church St., the
Churchill Arms pub is a hot local hangout with good beer
and decent £5 Thai plates. My favorite, the **Ladbroke Arms**,
serves £5 hot meals country-style daily from noon-2:30 p.m.
and 7:00-9:30 p.m. (indoor/outdoor, see map, 54 Ladbroke
Road, behind Holland Park Tube station, tel. 727-6648). The
almost-too-popular **Geale's** is one of London's best fish-
and-chips joints (2 Farmer Street, just off Notting Hill Gate
behind the Gate Theatre, noon-3:00 p.m., 6:00-11:00 p.m.,
closed Sunday, tel. 727-7969). Get there early for a place to
sit and the best selection of fish. The very English **Maggie
Jones** (6 Old Court Place, just east of Kensington Church
St., near the High Street Kensington tube stop, tel. 937-6462,
CC-VM) serves my favorite £20 London dinner. If you eat
well once in London, eat here.

BATH, ENGLAND'S COVER GIRL

Bath is Europe's most underrated city. Any tour of Britain that skips Bath stinks. Two hundred years ago, this city of 80,000 was the Hollywood of Britain. If ever a city enjoyed looking in the mirror, Bath's the one. It has more "government listed" or protected historic buildings per capita than any other town in England. The entire city, built of creamy warm-tone limestone called "Bath stone," beams in its cover-girl complexion. An architectural chorus line, it's the triumph of Georgian style. Proud locals remind visitors that the town is routinely banned from the "Britain in Bloom" contest to give other towns a chance to win. Bath's narcissism is justified.

Suggested Schedule

8:00	Breakfast.
9:00	Roman baths and museum, followed by an excellent 20-minute tour.
10:30	Take the city walking tour (depart in front of the Pump Room).
12:30	Your guide will probably end the tour at the Assembly Rooms. Browse downhill to find lunch.
3:00	Tour the #1 Royal Crescent Museum.
4:00	Catch tour of the Costume Museum in the Assembly Rooms.

Transportation: London to Bath

Trains leave at a quarter past each hour from London's Paddington station (75 minutes to Bath Spa, £25 one way). Direct National Express buses leave for Bath about every two hours from Heathrow airport (2½ hours). Consider using the all day Stonehenge and Bath organized bus tours from London as transportation. For the same cost of the train ticket (£25), you can see Stonehenge, tour Bath and leave the tour before it returns to London (they'll let you stow your bag underneath). Unless you have another sightseeing agenda, there's no reason to rent a car in

London just to drive it to Bath, try to find a parking place, and sightsee a day without using it. Cut two days off your rental by picking up your car in Bath after you've seen the city. Most major companies have offices in Bath and offer free hotel pick-ups.

National Express buses serve Bath well. For example, they go to and from: Gatwick airport (4½ hours, eight daily), Heathrow airport (2½ hours, nine daily), Oxford (2 hours, three daily), Stratford (2½ hours, two daily), and Cheltenham (2 hours, four daily). Tel. 0272/541022.

Orientation to Bath: Tourist Information is near the Abbey (Monday-Saturday 9:30 a.m.-6:00 p.m., Sunday 10:00 a.m.-4:00 p.m., shorter hours off-season, pick up the 25p Bath map/guide and the listings of sights and events, tel. 0225/462831). While everything worth your time is within enjoyable walking distance, consider using the Guide Friday "hop on and hop off" tour bus as transportation. It leaves every 12 minutes from lane one of the bus station, a block in front of the train station. My top three listings are on the line and farther than I'd want to walk with my bag. Start the tour, jump out, check into your B&B, and hop back on to finish the circle. A taxi from the station to the Royal Crescent costs about £2.50.

Sightseeing Highlights
▲▲**The "Guide Friday" City Bus Tour**—This green-and-cream open-top tour bus makes a 90-minute figure-eight circuit of Bath's main sights with an exhaustingly informative running commentary. For one £5 ticket, tourists can stop and go at will for a whole day. The buses cover the city center and the surrounding hills (14 sign-posted pick-up points, departures every 12 minutes in summer, hourly in winter, about 9:00 a.m.-6:00 p.m., tel. 0225/444102, children are often let on for free). This is great in sunny weather, a feast for photographers, and a fine way to work on a tan and sightsee at the same time. Consider the utilitarian value of this tour as pure transportation from the station to your hotel and onward.

▲▲▲**Walking Tours of Bath**—These 2-hour tours, offered free by trained local volunteers who simply want to share their love of Bath with its many visitors, are a pure, chatty, historical-gossip-filled joy, essential for your understanding of this town's amazing Georgian social scene. How else will you learn that the old "chair ho" call for your sedan chair evolved into today's "cheerio" greeting. Tours leave from in front of the Pump Room daily except Saturday at 10:30 a.m. (occasionally at 2:30 p.m. and 7:00 p.m., May-October).

▲▲▲**The Baths (Roman and Medieval)**—Back in ancient Roman times, high society enjoyed the mineral springs at Bath. Roman Londoners traveled to Aquae Sulis, as the city was called then, so often to "take a bath" that finally it became known as, simply, Bath. Today a fine Roman museum surrounds the ancient bath. With the help of an excellent 20-minute guided tour, the complex of ancient Roman and medieval baths and buildings makes sense. (£4; £5 "combo" ticket includes Costume Museum. Open 9:00 a.m.-6:00 p.m. daily, and 8:00 to 10:00 p.m. in August; shorter hours off-season. Tours are included and leave on the quarter-hour throughout the day.)

▲**Pump Room**—After a centuries-long cold spell, Bath was reheated when previously barren Queen Mary bathed here and ten months later bore a male heir to the throne (1687). Back on the aristocratic map, soon high society turned the place into one big pleasure palace. The Pump Room, an elegant Georgian Hall just above the Roman baths, offers the visitor's best chance to sample this Old World elegance. Drop by to sip coffee or tea to the rhythm of a string trio (tea and pastry for £2.25, live music all year 10:30 a.m.-1:00 p.m., summers 3:00-5:00 p.m.). Now's your chance to have a famous (but not especially good) "Bath bun" and (split a 35p) drink of the awfully curative water.

▲**The Abbey**—Bath town wasn't much in the Middle Ages. As late as 1687, there were only about 3,000 inhabitants gathered around its great abbey. But an important church has stood on this spot since Anglo-Saxon times. In 973, Edgar, the first king of England, was crowned here.

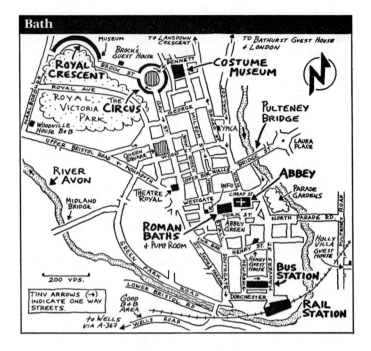

The present church, which dominates the town center, is 500 years old and a fine example of Late Perpendicular Gothic, with breezy fan vaulting and enough stained glass to earn it the nickname "Lantern of the West." (Evensong service and concert schedule is on the door, £1 donation).

Pulteney Bridge—Bath is inclined to compare its shop-lined bridge to Florence's Ponte Vecchio. That's pushing it. But to best enjoy a sunny Bath kind of day, pay 60p to go into the garden below the bridge. Tour boats run hour-long £3 cruises from under the bridge.

▲▲**Royal Crescent and The Circus**—Bath is an architectural can-can and these are the kickers. These first elegant Georgian (that's British for "neo-Classical") "condos" by John Wood are well-explained in the city walking tours. The museum at #1 Royal Crescent is your best look into a house from Jane Austen's day. Worth the £3 admission to get behind all those classy exteriors (daily 11:00 a.m.-5:00 p.m.).

▲▲▲**Costume Museum**—One of Europe's great museums, displaying 300 years of fashion one frilly decade at a time, is housed in Bath's elegant Assembly Rooms. Enthralling 45-minute tours will "knock your spots off" (normally leaving on the hour). Drop by or call to check tour times. Learn why Yankee Doodle "stuck a feather in his cap and called it macaroni," and much more (£2.50, cheaper on combo ticket with Roman Baths, daily 9:30 a.m.-6:00 p.m., shorter hours off-season, last tour often at 4:00 p.m., tel. 461111).

▲▲**The Industrial Heritage Centre** is a grand title for Mr. Bowler's Business, a turn-of-the-century engineer's shop, brass foundry and fizzy-drink factory. It's just a pile of meaningless old gadgets until a volunteer guide resurrects Mr. Bowler's creative genius (£2.80, plus a few pence for a glass of genuine Victorian lemonade, daily 10:00 a.m.-5:00 p.m., 2 blocks uphill from the Assembly Rooms on Julian Rd., call to be sure a volunteer is available to give a tour, tel. 318348).

Royal Photographic Society—Shutterbugs enjoy this museum, exhibiting the earliest cameras and photos and their development, along with temporary contemporary exhibits (£3, daily 9:30 a.m.-5:30 p.m.).

▲**American Museum**—I know, you need this in Bath like you need a Big Mac. But this offers a fascinating look at colonial and early-American lifestyles. Each of 18 completely furnished rooms (from the 1600s to the 1800s) is hosted by an eager guide waiting to fill you in on the candles, maps, bedpans, and various religious sects that make domestic Yankee history surprisingly interesting. One room is a quilter's nirvana (£5, Tuesday-Saturday 2:00-5:00 p.m., Sunday 11:00 a.m.-5:00 p.m., closed November-March. Outside of town and a headache to reach. A special museum bus leaves Bath daily in summer at 2:00, returning at 4:30. Otherwise it's a 15-minute walk from the Guide Friday circuit or a 10-minute walk from bus #18).

Entertainment—The TI's *This Month in Bath* lists events and evening entertainment. There are almost nightly historical walks (7:15 p.m., 2 hours). For a walking comedy act, you may enjoy the entertainingly off-the-wall "Bizarre Bath" walk (£3, 8:00 nightly, 75 minutes, from the Crystal Palace pub, confirm at TI). The Bath Sports and Leisure Centre (just across the North Parade Bridge, open until 10:30 p.m., tel. 462563) has a swimming pool and more.

Accommodations in Bath (£1 = about $1.50, tel. code: 0225)

Even with hotels advertising "recession prices," Bath is one of England's busiest tourist towns. To get a good B&B, make a telephone reservation in advance. Competition is stiff and it's worth asking any of these places for a non-weekend, three nights in a row, or off-season deal. My first four listings are on quiet streets.

Brock's Guest House: If you can afford the splurge, this Georgian townhouse will put bubbles in your Bath experience. Marion Dodd has redone her place in a way that would make the famous architect, John Wood, who built it in 1765, proud. This charming house couldn't be better located, between the prestigious Royal Crescent and the elegant Circus (S-£20, DB-£40 and £42, DBWC-£46 and £50, TB-£54, TBWC-£62; 32 Brock St., BA1 2LN, reserve far in advance, tel. and fax 338374). Marion serves a royal breakfast. You'll find a TV and teapot in your room, and a launderette around the corner. Like most listings in this book, she'll hold telephone reservations with no deposit until 3:00 p.m. (call if you'll be a little late). If Marion's place is full, she can set you up in a friend's B&B nearby. If you can't find a sedan chair, Marion is a 15-minute walk, £2.50 taxi, or short bus ride (to Assembly Rooms and short walk) from the station. Guide Friday buses stop on Brock Street.

In the **Woodville House**, Anne and Tom Toalster offer Bath's best cheap beds. This tidy little house has three charming rooms, one shared shower, a TV lounge, serves breakfast around one big family-style table, and "welcomes non-smokers" (S-£18, D-£26; just off busy Bristol Road below the Royal Crescent at 4 Marlborough Lane, BA1 2NQ, tel. 319335).

Holly Villa Guest House, with a cheery garden and a cozy TV lounge, an 8-minute walk from the station and center, is enthusiastically and thoughtfully run by Jill McGarrigle. (D-£34, DB-£38, DBWC-£44, T-£48, TB-£54, Q-£64, double rooms have double beds only, seven rooms, non-smoking, free parking, cheap rooms get the famous "loo with a view." From city center, walk over North Parade Bridge, take first right, then second left, a block from a Guide Friday bus stop, 14 Pulteney Gardens, BA2 4HG, tel. 310331.)

The Henry Guest House is a clean, cheery, and vertical, little eight-room family-run place 2 blocks in front of the train station on a quiet side street (S-£15, D-£30, T-£45, TVs in rooms, lots of narrow stairs, one shower and one W.C. for all; 6 Henry Street, BA1 1JT, tel. 424052, Mrs. Cox). This kind of decency at this price this central is found nowhere else in Bath. **Harington's of Bath Hotel**, on a quiet street in the town center, is sleepable in a pinch (D-£38, Queen Street, tel. 641728).

The Bathurst Guest House: Mrs. Elizabeth Tovey runs a fine B&B (S-£16, D-£32, DB-£37, extra bed-£8, non-smoking, TVs in rooms, lots of stairs, easy parking, 11 Walcot Parade, London Road, Bath BA1 5NF, tel. 421884) with a great piano/game lounge, 1 block above the A-4 London Road about a 15-minute walk north of the town center. The friendly **Claremont B&B** is farther out of town (D-£32, DB-£40, T-£50; 9 Claremont Rd., Bath, Diane Harding, tel. 428859).

For the cheapest beds, the **Youth Hostel** is in a grand old building, but not central (bus #18 from the station, £8.40 per bed without breakfast, tel. 465674). The **YMCA** is a bit grungy, but friendly and wonderfully central on Broad Street. Doubles are £12 per person; the dorm is cheaper at about £11, with breakfast (tel. 460471).

Eating in Bath

There's no shortage of fun places in all price ranges—just stroll around the center of town. A picnic dinner or take-out fish and chips in the Royal Crescent Park is ideal for aristocratic hobos.

On or just off the Abbey Green: Evans Self-Service Fish Restaurant (daily 11:30 a.m.-5:30 p.m., sometimes later, 7 Abbeygate, student discounts, tel. 463981) is the best eat-in or take-out fish and chips deal in town. The **Crystal Palace Pub**, with hearty meals under rustic timbers or in the sunny courtyard, is a good handy standby (meals under £5, daily from noon-2:30 p.m. and 6:00-8:30 p.m., 11 Abbey Green, children welcome on the patio, not indoors, tel. 423944). **Sally Lunn's House** is a cutesy quasi-historic place for expensive doily meals, tea, pink pillows, and lots of lace (4 North Parade Passage). **The Huntsman** (next to Sally Lunn's buns, tel. 460100) offers good, filling meals. Its pub is cheapest, the Cellar Bar is inexpensive and full of young locals, and the restaurant upstairs is a bit classier. For very cheap meals, try **Spike's Fish and Chips** (open very late) and the neighboring café just behind the bus station.

Between the Abbey and the Circus: For lunch, try **Lovejoy's Café** upstairs in the Bartlett Street Antique Centre or the **Green Tree Pub**, with a non-smoking room, on Green Street (both serve lunch only, downhill from the Assembly Rooms). The **Guildhall Market** near Pulteney Bridge, fun for browsing and picnic shopping, has a very cheap cafeteria if you'd like to sip tea surrounded by stacks of used books, bananas on the push list, and honest-to-goodness old-time locals. **The Broad Street Bakery** (at 14 Broad St.) is a budgetricious place with great quiches and pizzas to eat in or take away. **Devon Savouries** serves greasy, delicious take-out pasties; sausage rolls; and vegetable pies (on the main walkway between New Bond Street and Upper Borough Walls). **Sam Wellers Pub** serves good £5 dinners (open until 8:00 p.m., 14 Upper Borough Walls, tel. 466627).

Behind the Circus and Brock's Guesthouse: The Cedars Lebanese Restaurant (on a lane called Margaret's Buildings, just off Brock Street) serves an elegant have-it-all £12 "Cedars Mezze." A block or so away, the **Chequers Inn** (50 Rivers St.) is a smoky dive of a pub with cheap and finger-sticking disgusting grub.

Helpful Hints

There's great browsing between the Abbey and the Assembly Rooms. Shops close at 5:30 p.m., later on Thursdays.

Antiques? Tempting shops here and in the Cotswolds will overcharge you. For the best deal, pick up the local paper (usually out on Fridays) and shop with the dealers at estate sales and auctions listed in the "What's On" section.

When in need, the Pump Room's toilets are always nearby and open to the discreet public.

WELLS, GLASTONBURY, AVEBURY

Today, make a circle starting with the stone circle connoisseur's favorite, Avebury; to Glastonbury, steeped in legends of the Holy Grail and King Arthur; and to Wells, England's smallest cathedral city. Over-achievers could work in Stonehenge (but I'd go to any souvenir shop and see it on a post card).

Suggested Schedule	
8:30	Pick up tour or rental car and go to Avebury.
9:30	Explore Avebury.
11:00	Drive an hour to Glastonbury.
12:00	Tour Glastonbury Abbey, climb the tower, browse through the town.
3:30	Tour Wells Cathedral and town.
5:15	Evensong service in Cathedral, pub dinner, home late to Bath.

Transportation: Bath to Avebury (25 miles) to Glastonbury (56 miles) to Wells (6 miles) to Bath (20 miles)

This plan calls for 100 miles of driving. The roads are good, and the scenery between sites is okay, but not earth-shaking. Stick to the faster "A" roads to go as directly as possible. In Wells, park on the main square next to the tourist office, post office, and just about everything else. Glastonbury Abbey's parking lot is easy to find.

If you don't have a car, take a bus or an all-day tour. From Bath, buses run hourly to Wells (1½ hours). Transfer at Wells for Glastonbury (25 minutes). The most convenient, quickest way to see Avebury and Stonehenge without a car is to take a tour. Several reasonable all-day bus tours leave from Bath. Maddy Thomas's are cheapest and most fun (see below).

Sightseeing Highlights

▲▲**Glastonbury**—This place, located on England's most powerful line of prehistoric sights (called a ley line), gurgles with a thought-provoking mix of history and mystery. As you climb the legend-soaked conical hill called Glastonbury Tor, notice the remains of the labyrinth. In A.D. 37, Joseph of Arimathea brought vessels containing the blood and sweat of Jesus to Glastonbury, and with that, Christianity to England. While this is "proven" by fourth-century writings and accepted by the Church, the Holy Grail legend which sprang from this in the Middle Ages isn't. Many think the Grail trail ends at the bottom of the "Chalis Well," a natural spring at the base of the Glastonbury Tor.

In the twelfth century, England needed a morale-boosting folk hero for inspiration during a war with France. The fifth-century Celtic fort at Glastonbury was considered proof enough of the greatness of the fifth-century warlord Arthur. His supposed remains were dug up from the Abbey floor and Glastonbury Tor became woven into Arthurian legends.

The Glastonbury Abbey was England's most powerful in the tenth century. In the sixteenth century, Henry VIII, recognizing Glastonbury as a bastion of the church he fought, destroyed the Abbey. For emphasis, he hung and quartered the Abbot, sending the parts of his body to four different towns. Not to be kept down for more than a few centuries, Glastonbury rebounded. In an eighteenth-century tourism campaign, thousands signed affidavits stating that water from the Chalis Well healed them, and once again, Glastonbury was on the tourist map. Today Glastonbury and its Tor are a center for searchers, too creepy for the mainstream church, but just right for those looking for a place to charge their crystals. The Tor is seen by many as a Mother Goddess symbol.

Climb the Tor and visit Chalis Well at its base (great view, easy parking, always open), tour the Abbey (£2, open daily until 6:30 p.m., evocative ruins with an informative visitor center and a model of the church in the chapter house, tel. 04588/832267), and browse through the town. The Rainbow's End café (2 minutes from the Abbey on High Street) is a fine place for salads and new-age people-watching. If you're looking for a midwife or a

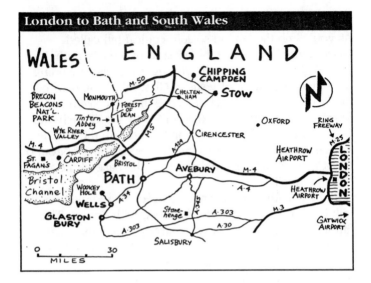

London to Bath and South Wales

male-bonding tribal meeting, read the notice board. (TI tel. 04588/32954.)

▲▲**Wells**—This wonderfully preserved little town has a cathedral, so it can be called a city. Its thirteenth-century cathedral is one of England's most interesting. Don't miss the carving on the west front, the unique hourglass-shaped double arch inside, or the grand chapter house (daily 7:15 a.m.-7:30 p.m., hour-long tours at 10:30, 11:00, 11:30, 2:00 and 2:30, good shop and a handy cafeteria). Weekdays (except Wednesday) at 5:15 and Sundays at 3:00, the cathedral choir takes full advantage of the place's heavenly acoustics with a 30-minute evensong service.

For a fine cathedral and town view from your own leafy hilltop bench, hike 10 minutes up Tor Hill. Lined with perfectly pickled fourteenth-century houses, the oldest complete street in Europe is Vicar's Close, 1 block north of the cathedral. Also next door is the moated Bishop's Palace (£2, open daily in August 11:00 a.m.-6:00 p.m.; April-October Tuesday and Thursday 11:00 a.m.-6:00 p.m. and Sunday 2:00-6:00 p.m.; closed winter).

If you're in the mood for a picnic, drop by the aromatic Cheese Board on the market square for a great selection of tasty local cheeses. Remember, Cheddar is just down the road. Ask the lady for a pound's worth of the most interesting mix. The Wells TI is on the Main Square (tel. 0749/672552).

Wells is so pleasant you might decide to spend the night. The Tor Guest House, with eight rooms in a seventeenth-century building facing the east end of the cathedral, is a good value (D-£32 to £38, DB-£35 to £45, cozy lounge and breakfast room, quiet, friendly, with car park; 20 Tor St., BA5 2US, tel. 0749/672322). The nearby Fountain Inn, on St. Thomas Street, is the best place for pub grub (fine curry, spareribs, and draft cider). The City Arms Pub is fun if you fancy grub in a former medieval jail.

▲**Wookey Hole**—This tacky commercial venture, worthwhile maybe as family entertainment, is a real hodgepodge. It starts with a wookey-guided tour of some big, but mediocre, caves complete with history, geology lessons, and witch stories. Then you're free to wander through a traditional rag paper-making mill with a demonstration, and into a nineteenth-century circus room—a riot of color, funny mirrors, and a roomful of old penny arcade machines that visitors can actually play for as long as their pennies (on sale there) last. They even have old girlie shows. (£5.20, daily May-September 9:30 a.m.-5:30 p.m., October-April 10:30 a.m.-4:30 p.m., 2 miles east of Wells, tel. 0749/672243.)

Wilkins Cider Farm—Scrumpy is the wonderfully dangerous local hard cider brewed in this part of England. The traditional old Wilkins Cider Farm, in Mudgeley near Wells, welcomes visitors. Apples are pressed from September through December. A half-gallon costs £2.15.

▲▲**Stonehenge**—England's most famous stone circle, with parts older than the oldest pyramid, was built between 3100 and 1100 B.C. These huge stones were brought all the way from Wales to form a remarkably accurate celestial calendar. Even today, every summer solstice (around June 21) the sun sets in just the right slot, and Druids go wild. The monument is roped off, so even if you pay the £2.70 entry fee, you're kept at a distance. You can see it free from the road (daily 10:00 a.m.-6:00 p.m.).

▲▲**Avebury**—The stone circle at Avebury is bigger (16 times the size), less touristy, and I think more interesting than Stonehenge. You're free to wander among 100 stones, ditches, mounds, and curious patterns from the past, as well as the village of Avebury, which grew up in the middle of this 1,400-foot-wide Neolithic circle. Fascinating.

Take the 1-mile walk around the circle. Visit the fine little archaeology museum (not the one on local farm life) and pleasant Stones café next to the National Trust store. The Red Lion Pub has good, inexpensive pub grub (tel. 06723/266). As you leave Avebury, notice the pyramid-shaped, manmade Silbury Hill. Nearly 5,000 years old, the largest manmade object in prehistoric Europe is a reminder that you've just scratched the surface of Britain's prehistoric and religious landscape.

▲▲**Maddy Thomas mini-bus tours**—If you don't have a car (or want to put off driving for a day), join Maddy Thomas on one of her £12 all-day six-to-12-person "Mad Max" minibus tours. Maddy thoughtfully organizes informative and inexpensive countryside excursions from Bath on most days. Her bus is old but reliable. Her schedule flexes according to demand. She picks up almost daily at 8:45 a.m. (at the statue on Cheap Street, behind Bath Abbey) for her basic all-day "Avebury, Stonehenge, and two cute villages (Lacock and Castle Combe)" tour. For the latest, get her schedule at the TI or call the hostel (0225/465674), Brock's Guest House (0225/338374), or 0926/842999. Upon request, she can do a great 1-day tour of Wells, Glastonbury, a scrumpy (cider) farm, and Avebury at a price a group of four would find cheap. For another personable local guide with a car or mini-bus, contact Roy Nicholls (Roy leads Best of Britain mini-bus tours for my company, Europe Through the Back Door, following the 22-day route laid out in this book) in Bath at tel. 0373/831311.

SOUTH WALES, FOLK MUSEUM, AND TO THE COTSWOLDS

From Bath, dash into South Wales' traditional past at St. Fagan's Welsh Folk Museum. Then take the scenic route past the romantic ruins of Tintern Abbey, up the lush Wye River Valley, through the quirky Forest of Dean, and into England's land of quaint—the Cotswold Hills—setting up in the centrally situated village of Stow-on-the-Wold or farther north in Chipping Campden.

Suggested Schedule

8:00	Breakfast.
8:45	Drive into Wales, past Cardiff.
10:00	St. Fagan's Welsh Folk Museum. Tour the grounds first, picnic, or lunch in cafeteria, then tour the museum gallery.
1:00	Drive to Tintern Abbey.
2:00	Explore Tintern, the Wye River, and the Forest of Dean.
5:00	Drive to the Cotswolds.
6:30	Set up in Stow or Chipping Campden.

Itinerary Option: If you need to save a day and aren't keen on folk museums, consider skipping South Wales entirely. The heart of the Cotswolds is a 90-minute drive from Bath.

Transportation: Bath to Cardiff (50 miles) to Tintern (40 miles) to Stow or Chipping Campden (60 miles)
Leave Bath following signs for A4, then M4, then Stroud. It's 10 miles north (on A46 past a village called Pennsylvania) to the M4 super-freeway. Now, only a speed reader can follow the map as you zip westward, crossing a huge suspension bridge into Wales. Twenty miles farther, just past Cardiff, take exit 33 and follow the brown signs south to the Welsh Folk Museum.

From St. Fagan's, the M4 and then M5 gets you to the Cotswolds in a hurry. For the scenic Tintern/Wye detour,

leave the M4 just before the big suspension bridge, taking
Chepstow exit #22, and follow signs up A466 to Tintern
Abbey and the Wye River Valley. Carry on to Monmouth
and, if you're running late, follow the A40 and the M50 to
the Tewksebury exit, where small roads will take you into
the Cotswolds.

If you have time and energy, explore the romantic old
Forest of Dean (info at the Tintern TI) through the beloved
old oak forest that made Admiral Nelson's ships so strong.

If you're using public transportation, catch a train to
Cardiff via Bristol (1¼ hours, hourly). City buses run
between Cardiff and the nearby Welsh Folk Museum.
From Cardiff, take a train to Cheltenham (1½ hours, every
two hours). Pick up the handy Cotswold Bus and Rail
Guide at the Cheltenham station (train info, 04525/29501,
bus info, 511655). From a public-transportation point of
view, Cheltenham is a good home base for the Cotswolds.
Another candidate is the village of Moreton-in-Marsh,
which has bus connections to Chipping Campden and a
train station on the Worcester-Oxford line.

Sightseeing Highlights
▲**Cardiff**—The Welsh capital has 300,000 people and a
pleasant modern center across from the castle. The castle
visit is interesting only if you catch one of the entertaining
tours (every half-hour). The interior is a Victorian fantasy.
▲▲▲**Welsh Folk Museum at St. Fagan's**—This best
look at traditional Welsh folk life displays more than
twenty carefully reconstructed old houses from all corners
of this little country. Each is fully furnished and comes
equipped with a local expert warming herself by the
toasty fire and happy to tell you anything you want to
know about life in this old cottage. Ask questions! You'll
see traditional crafts in action and a great gallery displaying crude washing machines, the earliest matches, elabo-
rately carved "love spoons," and even a case of memorabilia from the local man who pioneered cremation.
Everything is well explained (£3.50, daily 10:00 a.m.-5:00
p.m., closed winter Sundays, tel. 0222/569441).

St. Fagan's has three sections: houses, museum, and castle/garden. If the sky's dry, walk from old house to old house for 60 to 90 minutes, spend an hour in the large building's fascinating museum, skip the castle and gardens, and eat lunch in the museum's excellent, inexpensive cafeteria, the Vale Restaurant.

▲**Caerphilly Castle**—This impressive, but gutted, old castle, 30 minutes from the Welsh Folk Museum, is the second largest in Europe (after Windsor). With two concentric walls, it was considered to be a brilliant arrangement of defensive walls and moats. Notice how Cromwell's demolition crew tried to destroy it, creating the leaning tower of Caerphilly. (£1.75, daily 9:30 a.m.-6:30 p.m., shorter hours in winter. Since this 22-day tour covers other equally impressive fortresses in North Wales, I'd skip Caerphilly to make time for the scenic drive to Stow.)

▲**Tintern Abbey**—Just off the scenic A466 road in a lush natural setting, this poem-worthy ruined Abbey is worth a stop. (Helpful TI and shop with the useful Wye-Cotswolds map and Wales Tourist Board's *A Tourist Guide to North Wales* on sale.)

▲**Wye River Valley and Forest of Dean**—Lush, mellow, and historic, this region seduced me into an unexpected night in a castle. Local tourist brochures explain the Forest of Dean's special dialect, strange political autonomy, and its ties to Trafalgar and Admiral Nelson.

For a medieval night, check into the St. Briavels Castle Youth Hostel (members only, tel. 0594/530272). It's an 800-year-old Norman castle used by King John in 1215, the year he signed the Magna Carta, comfortable (as castles go), friendly, and in the center of the quiet village of St. Briavels just north of Tintern Abbey. For dinner, eat at the hostel or walk "just down the path and up the snyket" to the Crown Pub (good, cheap food and friendly pub atmosphere).

Accommodations in Stow-on-the-Wold (£1 = about $1.50, tel. code: 0451)

Stow-on-the-Wold is an ideal home base for the Cotswolds. Eight roads converge on Stow, but none interrupt the peacefulness of its main square. Stow has become a crowded tourist town but most are day-trippers, so even summer nights are peaceful. Stow has plenty of B&B options and a tourist office (tel. 0451/831082) on the main square. Parking on the square is free for two hours during the day. My first three listings are comfortable modern homes just out of town, a 5-minute walk from the square. The next three are old buildings right on the square. The last one is in a tiny village, a 10-minute drive away.

The Croyde B&B: Norman and Barbara Axon make you feel like part of the family. They offer two rooms, each with a double bed, in a pleasant, quiet, modern house with a garden, easy parking, and a warm and friendly welcome (D-£30, on Evesham Rd., Stow-on-the-Wold, Cheltenham, GL54 1EJ, tel. 831711). If my listings are full, Barbara can find you a good place elsewhere.

West Deyne B&B: Mrs. Joan Cave runs this cozy B&B with a peaceful garden overlooking the countryside on Lower Swell Road (double or twin-£28 with evening tea and biscuits, GL54 1LD, tel. 831011).

The Limes (D-£30, DB-£34, DBWC-£35, and family rooms, across the street from the Croyde B&B, on Evesham Rd., GL54 1EJ, tel. 830034) is run by Val Keyte, who's hosted travelers for nearly twenty years and serves a great breakfast.

The Pound: In her comfy, quaint, restored 500-year-old low-ceilinged, heavy-beamed home, Patricia Whitehead offers two spacious bright rooms with good strong twin beds and a classic old fireplace lounge (D-£32, right downtown on Sheep St., GL54 1AU, tel. 830229).

Stow Lodge Hotel, on the town square in its own sprawling and peaceful garden next to the church, is the best friendly, classy, old-hotel value. Thoughtfully appointed rooms in the main building are quieter and more characteristic than in the annex (D-£50, DB-£70, TB-£90, CC-A, no elevator, GL54 1AB, tel. 830485). This is a large, but family-run, hotel that somehow maintains a happy staff.

Stow-on-the-Wold Youth Hostel: On Stow's main square in a historic old building, with a friendly atmosphere, good hot meals served and a do-it-yourself member's kitchen, it's popular in summer. Call-in reservations are held until 6:00 p.m., or later with a credit card number (£6.30 per bed, £3.70 for dinner, tel. 830497). **Other Cotswold Youth Hostels** are in Cleve Hill (tel. 024267/2065) and Duntisbourne Abbots (tel. 0285821/682).

The Guiting Guest House: Six miles west of Stow in the tiny village of Guiting Power, this is your sleepy-village alternative. Mrs. Sylvester rents modern, delightfully doily rooms in her 400-year-old house (DB-£37, Post Office Lane, Guiting Power, Cheltenham, GL54 5TZ, tel. 0451/850470). Her husband is the local tourist board's B&B quality control man, so this place is either right on . . . or gets away with murder.

Accommodations in Chipping Campden (£1 = about $1.50, tel. code: 0386)

Nine miles north of Stow, Chipping Campden is more real. Not quite as touristy, it's a working market town, home of some incredibly beautiful thatched roofs and the richest Cotswold wool merchants ("Cotswold" comes from the Saxon phrase meaning "hills of sheeps' coats"). It's a few miles off the main road, to the north, and closer than Stow to Stratford (handy if you're going to a play one night).

Frances Cottage—Jill Slade rents two comfy rooms in her small home (DB-£32, £30 for stays of more than one night, one triple, non-smoking, narrow stairs, Lower High Street, GL55 6DY, tel. 840894).

Sparlings B&B—Those in search of aristocratic tidiness and grandfatherly clocks will sleep well in the very proper Mr. Black and Mr. Douglass' delightfully restored seventeenth-century stone town house. (D-£40, DB-£42, one night deposit required, peaceful garden, on High Street, GL55 6HL, tel. 840505).

Good Cotswold Pub Grub: In Stow, the formal but friendly bar in the Stow Lodge serves fine £5 lunches and £7 dinners (daily noon-2:00 p.m., 7:00-9:00 p.m.). Next

door, the **Queen's Head** serves an inexpensive decent
meal and the local Cotswold brew, Donnington Ale
(closed Monday). Near Stow, try dinner at **The King's
Head** in Bledington (moderate, closed Sunday). **The
Plough** in the hamlet of Cold Aston (a 10-minute drive
from Stow) is known for its good typical Cotswold food
and atmosphere.

In Chipping Campden, the **Volunteer Pub** is your best
cheap bet (Lower High Street, £5 lunch or dinner, 7:00-
9:00 p.m.). The **Badgers Wine Bar** serves better food
with less smoke for around £8 (in town center, on High
Street). For a lively local crowd and very likely a little
impromptu folk music, everyone loves the **Baker's Arms**
for dinner (closed Sunday, in Broad Campden, near
Chipping Campden). Since things change constantly, take
your B&B host's pub grub advice seriously.

THE COTSWOLD VILLAGES AND BLENHEIM PALACE

Today mixes England's coziest villages with her greatest countryside palace. The Cotswold Hills are dotted with storybook villages. The best are in the north a few minutes drive from Stow or Chipping Campden. England has plenty of royal country mansions. Visiting one is enough . . . as long as it's Blenheim.

Suggested Schedule

9:00	Joyride through Chipping Campden, Broadway, and Stanton, then drive via Cheltenham to Cirencester.
11:00	Cirencester—Corinium Museum, crafts center, lunch in crafts center's cafeteria.
1:00	Drive to Bibury via Coln St. Dennis, Coln Rogers, and Winson.
1:30	Bibury—stroll along the stream, see cottages and church.
2:30	Drive to Blenheim via Burford, Witney, and Woodstock.
3:15	Line up for the hour-long tour of Blenheim Palace.
5:15	Drive to Stow-on-the-Wold via Chipping Norton.
6:00	Evening stroll around Stow or Chipping Campden.
7:30	Find a good pub for dinner or see a Shakespeare play in Stratford.

Transportation

Although distances are very small in the Cotswolds, so are the roads (and public transportation schedules). Including the 20-mile drive to Blenheim on A4095, you'll probably put in 100 miles today—most of it as joyful as joyriding can be. Don't bumble around without a good map; any shop can sell you a fine, tourist-oriented map of the region. Peak season parking is a headache in tourist traps

like Broadway and Bourton. Blenheim Palace is in the
town of Woodstock on A34, 7 miles northwest of Oxford.
The palace turnoff is in Woodstock, not well sign-posted.
A "quick swing into Oxford" won't work: it has some of
England's worst traffic and parking problems. Today's
theme is cuteness. You'll find that best on the tiny roads.

Without a car, rent a bike or use the Cotswold Bus and
Rail Guide to plan your day. The train station nearest
Blenheim Palace is Hanborough, on the Worcester-Oxford
train line.

The Cotswolds

As with many fairy-tale regions of Europe, the present-day
beauty of the Cotswolds was the result of an economic
disaster. The area grew rich on the wool trade and built
lovely towns and houses. Then foreign markets stole their
trade and they slumped—too poor even to be knocked
down. The forgotten, time-passed villages in this 50-by-25-
mile piece of Gloucestershire have been rediscovered by
us twentieth-century romantics, and the Cotswold villages
are enjoying new prosperity.

Sightseeing Highlights

▲**Chipping Campden**—Chipping Campden is one of the
finest and richest of the old wool towns. Walk the full
length of High Street (its width indicates that it was a market town) and around the block at both ends. On one
end, you'll find impressively thatched homes on
Westington Street, past Sheep street, and on the other
end, a fine fifteenth-century perpendicular "wool" church
and a pleasant free memorial garden. Its pathetic/bizarre
tourist office is run out of the quirky "Woolstaplers' Hall
Museum" (wooden legs, old typewriters, jelly molds, and
the "largest collection of iron man-traps in Europe" in a
600-year-old building on High Street, TI and museum, daily
10:00 a.m.-5:00 p.m., tel. 0386/840289 or 840101). Drop by to
pay 5p for a town map. For accommodations, see Day 7.

▲**Stow-on-the-Wold**—Stow has no real sights other than
itself, a cutesy huddle of medieval pastel boutiques and
art galleries draped seductively around a big town-

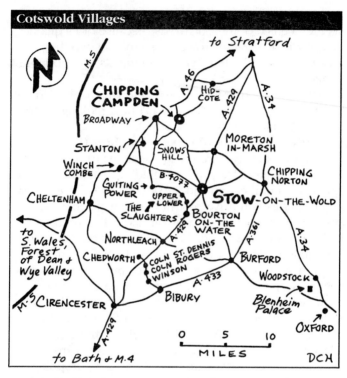

Cotswold Villages

N

to Stratford

M.5
A.46
CHIPPING CAMPDEN
HID-COTE
A.429
A.34
BROADWAY →
STANTON
SNOWS HILL
MORETON IN-MARSH
WINCH COMBE
B.4077
CHIPPING NORTON
GUITING POWER
UPPER LOWER
STOW-ON-THE-WOLD
CHELTENHAM
THE SLAUGHTERS
BOURTON ON-THE WATER
A.424
A.361
A.34
to S. Wales, Forest of Dean & Wye Valley
NORTHLEACH
CHEDWORTH
COLN ST. DENNIS
COLN ROGERS
WINSON
BURFORD
WOODSTOCK
M.5 CIRENCESTER
A.429
BIBURY
A.433
Blenheim Palace
OXFORD
to Bath & M.4
0   5   10
MILES
DCH

square/parking lot. There are several good pubs, some pleasant shops, and a handy little walking tour brochure called "Town Trail" (20p, sold at the TI and youth hostel). Follow the route, then lock your partner in the stocks on the green. For accommodations, see Day 7.

▲**Cirencester**—Nearly 2,000 years ago, this was the ancient Roman city of Corinium. It's 20 miles from Stow down A429, which was called Foss Way in Roman times. In Cirencester (towns ending in "cester" were Roman camps), stop by the Corinium Museum to find out why they say, "If you scratch Gloucestershire, you'll find Rome" (10:00 a.m.-6:30 p.m., Sunday 2:00-5:30 p.m., shorter hours and closed Monday off-season). The craft center and workshops entertain visitors with traditional weaving, baking, potting in action, an interesting gallery and a great coffee shop. Friday is market day in Cirencester (TI tel. 0285/654180).

Bourton-on-the-Water—I can't figure out if they call this the "Venice of the Cotswolds" because of its quaint canals or its miserable crowds. It's too cute, worth a drive-through and a few cynical comments, but no more (4 miles south of Stow).

Broadway—Another very crowded town, worth a drive-through but not a stop. There won't be a parking place anyway (9 miles northwest of Stow).

▲▲**Stanton, Upper and Lower Slaughter** (between Stow and Broadway), are my nominations for the cutest Cotswold villages. They're almost edible, each nestled in equally beautiful countryside. Ask your dad if you can sit on the roof as you drive past the stone walls, oaks and sheep nearby. Get out of your car and walk around.

▲**Bibury**—Six miles northeast of Cirencester, this is an entertaining, but money-grubbing and not very friendly, village with a trout farm, a Cotswolds museum, a stream teeming with fat trout and proud ducks, a row of very old weavers' cottages, and a church surrounded by rose bushes, each tended by a volunteer of the parish. Don't miss the scenic drive from A429 to Bibury through the villages of Coln St. Dennis, Coln Rogers, and Winson. Drivers might consider skipping Cirencester, dropping passengers in Coln Rogers for a pleasant 2-mile walk into Bibury where they, devoted drivers, will have an idyllic stream-bank picnic awaiting the walkers.

▲▲▲**Blenheim Palace**—Too many English palaces can send you into a furniture-wax coma, so this tour chooses just the best. The Duke of Marlborough's home, the largest in England, is still lived in. That is wonderfully obvious as you prowl through it. Churchill was born prematurely while his mother was at a Blenheim Palace party. The palace is well-organized with mandatory, excellent guided tours that leave every 10 minutes, last an hour, and cost £6. If you need more time in the excellent Churchill exhibit, skip to the next tour group (mid-March to October 10:30-5:30, last tour at 4:45, tel. 0993/811325). Churchill fans can visit his tomb in a nearby town.

▲**Woodstock**—Blenheim Palace sits at the edge of this cute town, stealing the show. For a half-timbered and memorable splurge, the Star Inn (DB-£45, CC-VMA, Market Place, tel. or fax 0993/811373), a 5-minute walk from the palace, is good for an overnight.

▲**Hidcote Manor**—If you like gardens, the grounds around this manor house are worth a look. These gardens, among the best in England, are at their fragrant peak in May, June, and July. (£4.50, 11:00 a.m.-7:00 p.m., n entry after 6:00 p.m., closed Tuesday and Friday, just past Chipping Campden.)

Itinerary Options

For a more leisurely day, skip Cirencester and Bibury. If it's Tuesday, drop by Moreton-in-Marsh for a lively, colorful market.

Consider renting a bike for a more intimate look at the Cotswolds where, according to some, two hours on two wheels is worth two days on four.

Without a car, some people find the Cotswolds a time-consuming mess. Speedy travelers can opt for a quick look at Castle Combe, the charming "southernmost Cotswold town," as a side-trip from Bath. (Bath TI has information on day tours.)

Remember, in Stow or Chipping Campden, you're just 30 minutes from Stratford, Shakespeare's birthplace. The world's best Shakespeare is performed by the Royal Shakespeare Company there and in London. You should reserve your tickets in advance (see London Entertainment) but there are often tickets available at the door.

If you'd prefer Oxford to Cambridge (which is reasonable, though I don't), you can do it as a side trip from London or the Cotswolds. Consider an extra day in the itinerary here, which would give you a whole day in the Cotswolds and a day split between Blenheim and Oxford (11:00 a.m. Blenheim tour, in Oxford by 1:00 p.m.; go straight to the tourist office to reserve a spot on an afternoon walking tour).

STRATFORD-UPON-AVON AND WARWICK CASTLE TO IRONBRIDGE GORGE

Today's drive into the cradle of the Industrial Revolution is a hopscotch of interesting sights. Spend the morning touring Shakespeare's birthplace at Stratford. Explore England's greatest medieval castle in Warwick, then after a possible stop in Coventry, zoom (hopefully) through England's second largest city, Birmingham, into the Severn River valley. Once churning with industry, this is now a land of sleepy smokestacks, soothing natural beauty, and a distinct Shropshire brand of hospitality.

Suggested Schedule

9:00	Leave Stow or Chipping Campden.
9:30	Park in Stratford, catch the Guide Friday tour with possible stops at Mary Arden's House or Anne Hathaway's Cottage.
11:00	Visit Shakespeare's house.
12:00	Drive to Warwick, picnic at the castle.
1:00	Tour the Warwick castle.
3:00	Drive to Ironbridge Gorge.
4:30	Arrive in Ironbridge Gorge (get a possible head start on tomorrow's sightseeing).

Transportation: Stow to Stratford (20 miles) to Warwick (8 miles) to Coventry (10 miles) to Ironbridge (56 miles)

Today's sights are close together and served by fine and well-marked roads. Entering Stratford, you cross a bridge. Veer right (following "P," Wark, and Through Traffic signs) and park in the multi-story garage (50p, 2 hours, you'll find nothing easier or cheaper). The TI and Guide Friday bus stop is a block away. Theaters and Shakespeare's house are 4 blocks away.

Leaving the garage, circle right around the same block, but stay on the "Wark" (Warwick, A46) road. Warwick is 8 miles away. The castle is just south of town on the right. After the castle, carry on through the center of Warwick,

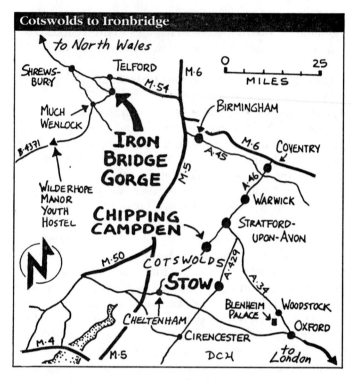

Cotswolds to Ironbridge

following signs to Coventry (still A46). If stopping in Coventry, follow signs painted on the road into the "city centre" and then to the cathedral parking. Grab a place in the high-rise car park. Leaving Coventry, follow signs to Nuneaton and M6 North through lots of sprawl and you're on your way. The M6 threads through giant Birmingham. This plan hits rush hour, but it doesn't seem to be a problem. From M6, take M54 to the Telford/Ironbridge exit. Following the Ironbridge signs, you do-si-do through a long series of roundabouts until you're there.

Buses connect Cheltenham, Stratford, Warwick, and Coventry pretty well (tel. 0788/535555); for example, Stratford-Warwick (20 minutes, bus and train almost hourly) and Warwick-Coventry (75 minutes, bus almost hourly). Frequent trains go to and from the region's hub, Birmingham. But transportation to and around Ironbridge is so bad, I'd skip it without a car. For the diehards: Take a train from Birmingham's New Street station to Telford (45 minutes, hourly), walk 15 minutes to the Telford bus station, and catch a bus to Ironbridge, 7 miles away.

Sightseeing Highlights in and near Stratford-upon-Avon
▲▲**Shakespeare's Birthplace**—Stratford is the most overrated tourist magnet in England, but you're passing through, and nobody back home would understand if you skipped Shakespeare's house. In the town center (address unnecessary, follow crowds), this half-timbered Elizabethan building is furnished as it was when young William grew up there and is filled with bits about the life and work of the great dramatist (£2.50, 9:00 a.m.-6:00 p.m., from 10:00 a.m. on Sunday, shorter hours in winter).

Shakespeare's hometown is blanketed with opportunities for "bardolotry." There are four other "Shakespearian Properties," all run by the Shakespeare Birthplace Trust, in and near Stratford. **Anne Hathaway's Cottage,** a mile out of town in Shottery, is a picturesque thatched cottage in which the bard's wife grew up. Much more than a "cottage," it's a 12-room farmhouse that has little to do with Shakespeare, but offers an intimate peek at lifestyles in Shakespeare's day. Guides in each room do their best to lecture to the stampeding hordes. **Mary Arden's House,** the girlhood home of William's mom, is in Wilmcote, about 3 miles from town. This sixteenth-century farmhouse sees far fewer tourists, so the guides in each room have a chance to do a little better guiding. A nineteenth-century farming exhibit and a falconry demonstration are on the grounds (both houses, about the same hours and price as His birthplace).

▲▲**Guide Friday Stratford Tours**—These open-top buses constantly make the rounds, allowing visitors to hop in and hop off at every sight in town. The full circuit takes about an hour and comes with a steady and informative live commentary (£6, buses every 15 minutes from 9:30, less frequent off-season, tel. 0789/294466). For a very quick stop, just catch this tour near the TI and car park, and visit the birthplace.

▲▲**Walking Tour**—A far better value than touring the various Shakespeare buildings, a guided walk makes this historic, but oversold, town endearing. Tours are scheduled only on Sundays at 10:30 (£2), but private tours are affordable for small groups. Call Mrs. Pat Bouverat at 0789/269890.

The World of Shakespeare is a gimmicky, but fun, look at Elizabethan and Renaissance England (£3, 9:30-9:30 in summer, until 5:30 in winter, shows on the half hour, 25-minute show, between the big Theatre and the bridge/TI, tel. 0789/269190).

▲▲**Royal Shakespeare Company**—The RSC, undoubtedly the best Shakespeare Company on earth, splits its season between London and Stratford. If you're a Shakespeare fan, see if the RSC schedule fits into your itinerary either in London or on one of your Cotswold nights. Tickets range from £8 to £22 (Monday-Saturday at 7:30 p.m., Thursday and Saturday matinees at 1:30 p.m., Hamlet starts an hour earlier). You'll probably need to buy your tickets in advance, although 50 seats are saved to be sold each morning, and unclaimed tickets can often be picked up the evening of the show (box office tel. 0789/295623, 24-hour ticket availability information tel. 0789/269191). Theater tours are given most days at 1:30 and 5:30, but not on matinee days. Over a thousand RSC paintings, props and costumes are on display (9:15 a.m.-8:00 p.m., Sunday noon-5:00 p.m.). The Shakespeare Connection is a convenient rail/bus shuttle for Stratford playgoers sleeping in London (2½ hours each way, £25 round-trip).

▲▲**Warwick Castle**—England's finest medieval castle is almost too groomed and organized, giving its hordes of visitors a good value for the steep £6.75 entry fee. With a lush green grassy moat and fairy-tale fortification, Warwick will entertain you from dungeon to lookout. There's something for every taste—a fine and educational armory, a terrible torture chamber, a knight in shining armor posing on a horse, a Madame Tussaud re-creation of a royal weekend party with an 1898 game of statue-maker, and a grand garden and peacock-patrolled, picnic-perfect park (daily 10:00 a.m.-6:00 p.m., 80-minute cassette tape tours for £1.50, sandwiches on sale in park, best castle eatery is The Stables near the turnstile, tel. 0926/445421).

▲**Coventry's Cathedral**—The Germans bombed Coventry to smithereens in 1940. From that point on, the German word for "to really blast the heck out of a place" was to "coventrate." But Coventry left smithereens, and its message to our world is one of forgiveness and reconciliation. The symbol of Coventry is the bombed-out hulk of its old cathedral with the huge new one adjoining it. The inspirational complex welcomes visitors. Climb the tower (£1, 180 steps). If you're touring the church, first see the 18-minute movie, The Spirit of Coventry, downstairs (£1.25 for the movie, plus a requested donation at the church door, 9:30 a.m.-5:00 p.m., Sunday 11:30-3:30, tel. 0203/227597).

Coventry's most famous hometown girl, Lady Godiva, rode bareback through the town in the eleventh century to help lower taxes. You'll see her bronze statue a block from the cathedral (near Broadgate). Just beyond that is the Museum of British Road Transport (first, fastest, and most famous cars and motorcycles from this British "Detroit"). If you stop in Coventry, take an opportunity to browse through the closest thing to normal workaday urban England you'll see on this route.

Accommodations in Ironbridge Gorge (£1 = about $1.50, tel. code: 0952)
The Hill View Farm—While Rosemarie Hawkins runs a peaceful, clean, friendly farmhouse B&B, her husband John raises a "beef suckler herd." Walk around the farm. Beware of the gander. If you're looking for calm and country, this is it, in a great rural setting overlooking the ruins of a twelfth century abbey (S-£16, double-£30, twin-£32; Buildwas, Ironbridge, Shropshire, TF8 7BP; tel. 432228). The Hawkins' farm is halfway between Ironbridge and Much Wenlock on A4169; leave Ironbridge past the huge modern power plants (coal), cross the bridge, and go about a mile. You'll see the sign.

The Library House is "better homes and castles" elegant. In the town center, right across from the bridge, it's classy but friendly, and a fine value. Chris and George Maddocks run a smoke-free place. Their breakfast won a "healthy heartbeat" award. (DB-£44, TB-£55; 11 Severn Bank, 1B, Shropshire TF8 7AN, tel. 432299, easy telephone reservations, they can reserve a table for you at the Coracle restaurant, parking passes available.)

The Wharfage Cottage is not cramped but cozy, a comfy three-bedroom place with ancient beams and color TVs, run by Pat Sproson (D-£36, DB-£38, TB-£50, QB-£56; 17 the Wharfage, TF8 7AW, on "main street," 2 minutes from the bridge, easy parking, tel. 432721).

Severn Lodge offers three rooms in an 1832 captain of industry mansion with a sit-a-spell garden and views of the lush hills (but not of the river where the sweatshops used to groan). This spacious place has all the hotel extras and easy parking. Carefully playing by the tourist board rules, Mrs. Reed won the coveted "Deluxe" (top 1%) category. (Twin or double with the works-£44; from the Wharfage Cottage, go 1 block up the small steep New Road, Ironbridge, Shropshire, TF8 FAX, tel. and fax 432148).

Woodlands Farm is an adventure in budget sleeping. When local workers aren't housed here, the musty, shaggy-carpeted, but sleepable, place offers the cheapest beds in town (S-£10, D-£20, T-£30, with an English breakfast, from the IBG Museum's Visitor Centre, take the steep little road about a mile, Beech Road, tel. 432741). The farm runs a private fishing business, Beeches Pool, where only barbless hooks are used and locals toss their catch back to hook again (kind of a fish hell).

Ironbridge Gorge Youth Hostel—Built in 1859 as the Coalbrookdale Institute, this grand building is now a fine hostel (a 20-minute walk from the Iron Bridge down A4169 toward Wellington, £9 beds with sheets in 4- to 6-bed rooms, £4 dinners, closed from 10:00 a.m.-5:00 p.m., tel. 433281, easy telephone reservations).

Wilderhope Manor Youth Hostel—This beautifully remote and haunted 500-year-old manor house is one of my favorite youth hostels anywhere in Europe. One day a week, tourists actually pay to see what we youth hostelers sleep in for £7.50. Closed Sunday night. It's 6½ miles from Much Wenlock down B4371 toward Church Stretton. Evening meals are served at 7:00 p.m. (Tel. 0694/771363.)

Eating in Ironbridge Gorge:

The Coracle Restaurant, run by Mr. and Mrs. Prichard, is every local's favorite place for a special evening out (£7 dinners, 7:00-9:30 p.m., reservations normally necessary, town center, near the bridge, tel. 433913). Downstairs, Peter and Paul run Oliver's, a delightful smoke-free vegetarian place.

For a pleasant evening, drive down Wenlock Edge on B4371. At Wenlock Edge Inn, park and walk to the cliff for a marvelous view of Shropshire at sunset. For dinner, eat at the inn, or better, drive 4 miles farther to Cardington and eat at the Royal Oak, a real country pub. Also good are the entertaining George and Dragon Pub and the Talbot Pub, in Much Wenlock.

IRONBRIDGE GORGE MUSEUMS–NORTH WALES

Go from the gritty pits of England's industrial infancy to the poetic hills of remote northern Wales. The Industrial Revolution started in England's Severn River Valley. Today, the Ironbridge Gorge is preserved as a showcase of the days that powered Britain to the pinnacle of the industrial world. In its glory days, this now-drowsy valley gave the world the first iron wheels, steam-powered locomotive, and cast-iron bridge.

Suggested Schedule

8:30	Breakfast
9:30	Iron Bridge, town, shops.
10:00	Visit the Museum of the River and Visitors' Centre, introduction video, exhibit.
11:00	Museum of Iron and Darby's furnace (or go directly to Blists Hill).
12:00	Blists Hill Open-Air Museum, picnic, cafeteria or pub lunch.
3:30	Drive to Wales.
4:30	Llangollen, 30-minute stop in town or at abbey.
5:00	Horseshoe Pass Road to Ruthin.
6:00	Check into your Ruthin B&B.
7:30	Medieval Banquet at Ruthin Castle.
11:00	Find your way home.
12:00	Still not home? More mead!

Sightseeing Highlights—Ironbridge

▲▲▲**Ironbridge Gorge Industrial Revolution Museums**—Start with the Iron Bridge. The first ever (1779), this is the area's centerpiece, open all the time and free.

The Museum of the River and Visitors' Centre, in the Severn Warehouse 500 yards upstream, is the orientation center. Be here at 10:00 a.m. when it opens to see the 10-minute introductory movie, check out its exhibit and model of the gorge in its heyday, and buy your guidebook

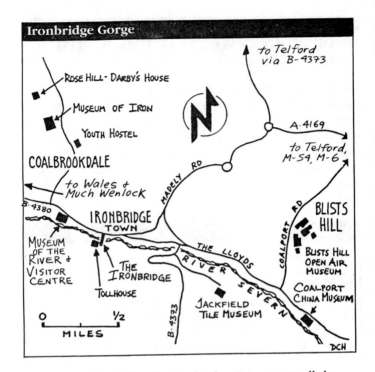

Ironbridge Gorge

and tickets (£7.80 for the Ironbridge Passport to all the sights, £5.50 for Blists Hill only).

Just up the road in Coalbrookdale, you'll find the Museum of Iron (worth a quick look) and Abraham Darby's blast furnace (inside a glass pyramid). This is the birthplace of the Industrial Revolution where, in 1709, Darby first smelted iron using coke as fuel. If you're like me, "coke" is a drink and "smelt" is the past tense of smell, but this event kicked off the modern industrial age.

Save most of your time and energy for the great Blists Hill Open-Air Museum—50 acres of Victorian industry, factories, and a re-created community from the 1890s, complete with Victorian chemists, an ancient dentist's chair, candlemakers, a working pub, a fascinating squatter's cottage, and a snorty, slipslidey pigsty. Take the lovely walk along the canal to the "inclined plane," have a picnic, or lunch in the Victorian Pub or the cafeteria near the squatter's cottage. The £1.25 Blists Hill guidebook gives a good step-by-step run-down (daily 10:00 a.m.-5:00 p.m., maybe until 6:00 p.m. in summer, tel. 0952/433522 on weekdays, 432166 on weekends). In July and August there may be a cheap shuttle bus between all sights; otherwise, those without wheels are in for a walk.

The TI office is a block from the Iron Bridge (8:45 a.m.-6:00 p.m., weekends from 10:00 a.m., off-season closing at 5:00 p.m., tel. 0952/432166).

Transportation: Ironbridge to Ruthin, North Wales (60 miles)

Most of the day is spent at easy-to-find museums within a few miles of the Iron Bridge. In mid-afternoon, drive for an hour to Wales via A5 through Shrewsbury, crossing into Wales at the pretty castle town of Chirk. There, take A5 to Llangollen. Cross the bridge in Llangollen, turn left, and follow A542 and A525 past the romantic Valle Crucis Abbey, over the scenic Horseshoe Pass, and into Ruthin.

If you're using public transportation, get on the Birmingham-Shrewsbury train (1 hour, nearly hourly), transfer at Shrewsbury, and take the train to Wrexham (40 minutes, every 2 hours). Pick up a North Wales bus and train schedule at the station, and ask about Rover and Ranger passes. From Wrexham, catch a bus to Ruthin via Mold (2 hours, hourly).

Sightseeing Highlights—North Wales

▲**Llangollen**—Well worth a stop, Llangollen is famous for its musical International Eisteddfod (for six days starting the first Tuesday in July; July 5-10 in 1994), a festival of folk songs and dance, very popular—and crowded. You can walk or ride a horse-drawn boat down its old canal (£3, 45 minutes round-trip, tel. 0978/860702) toward the lovely thirteenth-century Cistercian Abbey (£1.50) near the even older cross called Eliseg's Pillar. (TI tel. 0978/860828.)

▲**Ruthin**—The ideal home base for your exploration of North Wales, Ruthin (pronounced "rith-in") is a market town serving the scenic Vale of Clwyd (pronounced "klu-id"). The TI office (daily 10:00 a.m.-5:30 p.m. in sum-

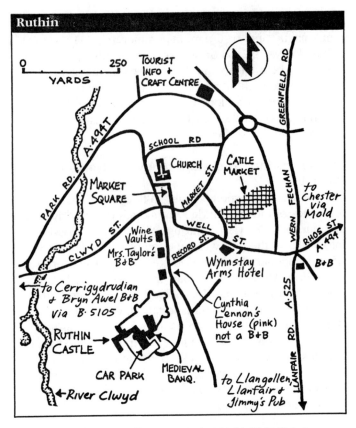

mer, shorter hours off-season, tel. 0824/703992) is in a
busy crafts center with 13 working shops, a gallery, and a
fine cafeteria.

▲▲**The Ruthin Castle Welsh Medieval Banquet**—This
"medieval banquet" is a touristy gimmick—but a fun one.
For one crazy evening, take a romanticized trip into the
bawdy Welsh past. English, Scottish, Irish, and Welsh
medieval banquets are all variations on the same theme.
This one is more tasteful and less expensive than most,
and it plays right into our 22-day plan.

You'll be greeted with a chunk of bread dipped in salt
which the maiden explains will "guarantee your safety."
Your medieval master of ceremonies then seats you, and
the evening of food, drink, and music rolls gaily on. Harp

music, angelic singing, wenches serving mead, spiced wine, four hearty traditional courses eaten with your fingers and a dagger, bibs, candlelight, pewter goblets, and lots of entertainment including insults slung at the Irish, Scots, English, and even us brash colonists. (£23, vegetarian options, starts at 8:00 p.m., runs most nights depending upon demand, down Castle Street from the town square, easy doorstep parking, CC-VMA, call in a reservation, tel. 0824/703435.)

▲**Welsh Men's Choir**—For an informal evening of great Welsh singing, visitors are welcome at the Hand Hotel (inexpensive pub dinners, but don't sleep here, tel. 0978/860303) in Llangollen, a 30-minute drive from Ruthin. Practice sessions start at 7:30 p.m. on Monday and Friday, followed by a sing-along in the pub at 9:00. Warning: the hotel may be filled with large tour groups.

Accommodations in Ruthin (£1 = about $1.50, tel. code: 0824)

Bryn Awel—Beryl and John Jones run a warm, traditional, charming farmhouse B&B in the hamlet of Bontuchel just outside of Ruthin (double or twin-£32, £34 for one nighters, tel. 702481). Beryl is an excellent cook, and eager to help you with touring tips and a few key Welsh words. She can call and reserve the medieval banquet for you. From Ruthin, take the Bala road, #494, then the B5105 Cerrigydrudion Road. Turn right after the church, at the Bontuchel/Cyffylliog sign. Bryn Awel is on the right, 1½ miles down the little road. Go to the Bridge Hotel and backtrack 200 yards.

Eleanor Jones' B&B is in a cozy fifteenth-century Tudor home near the castle, town square, and bus stop. This place, with a library, grand piano, and royal breakfast, is a downtown gem (three huge rooms, £14.50 per person, 8a Castle Street, tel. 702748).

The Wine Vaults is a musty old inn right on Ruthin's main square, run by Mrs. Taylor, with a pub downstairs. This is the most central location possible, but less cozy than a B&B (four doubles or twins-£30, tel. 702067).

Eyarth Station, a well-run modern home in what used to be a train station, is set peacefully in the countryside a mile south of Ruthin (£18 per person, Llanfair D.C., LL15 2EE, tel. 703643, Jen and Albert Spencer).

Margaret Rauson's B&B, (Rhianfa, Fjordd Llaurhydd, Ruthin, Clwyd. LL15, 1PP, near hospital, tel. 0824/702971, no smoking), in a big brick home, is friendly, comfortable, and moderately priced.

The Ruthin Castle is the ultimate in creaky Old World elegance for North Wales. But, at £82 per double, it's a serious splurge. (Tel. 702664.)

For inexpensive dorm beds, you'll need to go to the Llangollen youth hostel (15 miles from Ruthin, tel. 0978/860330). Four miles outside of Ruthin on the A525 road, the Llysfasi Agricultural College rents out student dorms in the summer (£12 per bed in singles or doubles, with breakfast, tel. 097/888263).

Eating in Ruthin

The **Anchor Pub** is fairly expensive, with good food. **The Cross Keys Inn**, just west of town, is a friendly Ruthin pub serving excellent meals. Also consider the **Manor House Hotel Restaurant** for a moderate dinner. The **Chardonney's Wine Bar** and **Eagles Pub**, in the town center, both serve good pub grub. The cafeteria in the crafts center next to the TI is bright and cheery.

EXPLORING NORTH WALES

Today's sightseeing menu is a real Welsh stew: a tour of Caernarfon, North Wales' mightiest castle; one of the world's largest slate mines at Blaenau Ffestiniog; and some of Britain's most beautiful scenery in the Snowdonia National Park, from the towering Mount Snowdon to lush forests to desolate moor country.

Suggested Schedule

9:00	Drive to Caernarfon with short stops in Trefriw Mill, Betws-y-Coed (information center, shops, waterfalls), and over Llanberis Mountain Pass.
12:00	Caernarfon Castle. Catch noon tour, 1:00 movie in Eagle Tower.
1:30	Climb to top for view.
2:00	Walk through town, shop, see Regimental Museum or Prince Charles (of Wales) exhibit in the castle.
2:30	Drive the scenic road to Blaenau Ffestiniog.
3:30	Tour Llechwedd Slate Mine.
5:30	Drive home.
7:00	Arrive back in Ruthin.

Transportation: Ruthin to Caernarfon (56 miles) to Blaenau (34 miles) to Ruthin (35 miles)
Every road in North Wales has its charm, but this day includes the best—lots of scenic wandering on small roads. From Ruthin, take B5105 (the steepest road off the main square) and follow the signs to Cerrigydrudion. Then follow A5 into Betws-y-Coed with a possible quick detour to the Trefriw Woolen Mill (3 miles north on B5106, well signposted). Continue west on A5 to Capel Curig, then take A4086 over the rugged Pass of Llanberis, just under the summit of Mt. Snowdon (to the south, behind those clouds), and on to Caernarfon. Park under the castle (very central) in the harbor-side car park.

Leaving Caernarfon, take the lovely A4085 southeast through Beddgelert to Penrhyndeudraeth. (Make things even more beautiful by taking the little B4410 road from Garreg through Rhyd.) Then take A487 toward Maentwrog, and A496 to Blaenau Ffestiniog. Go through the dark, depressing mining town of Blaenau Ffestiniog on A470 until you wind up in the hills of slate and turn right into the Llechwedd Slate Mine.

After the mine, A470 continues north on the most scenic stretch of all (past a ruined castle and several remote, intriguing B&Bs) through Dolwyddelan and back to A5. For a high and desolate detour, return to Ruthin via the windy, windy (curvy, blowy) A543 road over the stark moors to the Sportsmans Arms Pub (the highest pub in Wales, good food).

If you're using public transportation, catch a bus from Ruthin to Rhyl (1¼ hours, hourly). Take the train west to Llandudno Junction (20 minutes twice hourly), and either transfer south to Betws-y-Coed (30 minutes, every 2 hours) and Blaenau Ffestiniog (30 more minutes), or continue west to Bangor (25 minutes), where you can catch a bus south to Caernarfon (25 minutes, four hourly).

Sightseeing Highlights

Betws-y-Coed—This is the resort center of Snowdonia National Park, bursting with tour buses and souvenir shops. It has a good National Park and Tourist Information office (tel. 0690/710426). The main street is worth a walk.

As you drive west out of town on A5, you'll see the car park for scenic Swallow Falls, a 5-minute walk from the road. A mile or so past the falls, on the right, you'll see "The Ugly House," built overnight to take advantage of a fifteenth-century law that let any quickie building avoid fees and taxes.

Trefriw Woolen Mills—The mill in Trefriw, 3 miles north of Betws-y-Coed, is free and surprisingly interesting (Monday-Friday 9:00 a.m.-noon and 2:00-5:30 p.m., tel. 0492/640462). Follow the 11 stages of wool manufacturing—warping, weaving, carding, hanking, spinning, and so on; then enjoy the fine woolen shop, pleasant town (more so than Betws-y-Coed), and coffee shop.

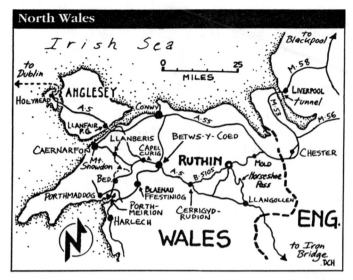

North Wales

▲▲**Caernarfon Castle**—Edward I built this impressive castle 700 years ago to establish English rule over North Wales. It's a great castle, all ready to entertain. Watch the movie (on the half-hour in the Eagle Tower); climb the Eagle Tower for a great view; take the guided tour (50-minute tours for £1 leave on the hour from the center of the courtyard in front of entry—if you're late, ask to join one in progress); and see the special exhibit on the investiture of Prince Charles and earlier Princes of Wales (£3.50, daily 9:30 a.m.-6:30 p.m., winter 9:30 a.m.-4:00 p.m., Sunday 2:00-4:00 p.m., tel. 0286/677617).

Caernarfon is a great town, bustling with shops, cafés, and people. The TI across from the castle entrance (tel. 0286/672232) can nearly always find you an inexpensive B&B. The Isfryn B&B is a good value (D-£30, DB-£35, family deals, 11 Church St., tel. 0286/675628). It's just down the street from the castle, overlooking the water.

▲▲**Llechwedd Slate Mine Tour**—Slate mining played a huge role in Welsh heritage, and this mine on the northern edge of the bleak mining town of Blaenau Ffestiniog does its best to explain the mining culture of Wales. This is basically a romanticized view of the depressing existence of the Welsh miners of the Victorian age who mined

and split most of the slate roofs of Europe. For every ton
of usable slate found, 10 tons are mined. Wales has a
poor economy, so touristizing slate mines is understand-
able. (daily 10:00 a.m.-6:00 p.m., closing at 5:00 p.m. in
winter, two tours offered—the "deep mine" tour features
the social life, the tramway focuses on the working life—
£4.50 for one tour or £7 for both. Dress warmly and don't
miss the slate-splitting demonstration, open to all, at the
end of the tramway tour. Tel. 0766/830523.)

Blaenau Ffestiniog is the quintessential Welsh slate-mining
town (TI tel. 0766/830360). The Fron Heulog guest house
is friendly, offers discount coupons to the mines, and can
point you towards a chapel where the men's choir
rehearses (D-£25, High Street, tel. 0766/831790, Keith
and Liz Thomasson).

Helpful Hints
The Welsh language is alive and well. In a pub, impress
your friends (or make some) by toasting the guy who
might have just bought your drink. Say "Yeach-hid dah"
(meaning "Good health to you") and "Dee olch" (Thank
you), or "Dee olch un vowr" (Thanks very much). If the
beer's bad, just make something up.

BLACKPOOL, ENGLAND'S CONEY ISLAND

Today you'll go from God's glorious garden to man's tacky, glittering strip-mall of fun, from pristine North Wales to the bells and blinkers of Blackpool. Blackpool, a middle-sized city with a 6-mile beach promenade, is ignored by guidebooks (*Let's Go: Britain*, in 570 pages of small print, never even mentions Blackpool). Even the most thorough bus tour will show you castles till your ears crenelate, but will never take an American visitor to Blackpool.

This is Britain's fun puddle, where every Englishman goes but none will admit it. It's England's most-visited attraction, the private domain of its working class and a favorite of kids of any age. When I told Brits I was Blackpool-bound, their expression soured and they asked, "Oh God, why?" Because it's the affordable escape of North England's Anne and Andy Capps. It's an ears-pierced-while-you-wait, tipsy-toupee kind of place. Tacky, yes. Lowbrow, okay. But it's as English as can be, and that's what you're here for. The plan is to enjoy a slow morning in Ruthin, drive 2 hours, get set up, and spend the rest of the day just "muckin' about" (British for "messin' around"). If you're bored in Blackpool, you're just too classy.

Itinerary Option: Actually, Wally World's frumpy mother, Blackpool, is a scary thing to recommend. Many people

Suggested Schedule

9:00	Breakfast, slow morning.
10:00	Ruthin, free time, craft center, shopping.
11:00	Drive to Blackpool.
1:00	Arrive in Blackpool. Visit TI (follow signs) and set up in a B&B, buy show ticket, catch a trolley to the South Pier.
2:00	Pleasure Beach.
4:30	The Blackpool Tower.
7:30	Music Hall Variety Show.
10:00	Prowl through the night lights, crowds, one-armed bandits, pubs, and clubs of England's Coney Island.

(ignoring the "50 million flies can't all be wrong" logic) think I overrate Blackpool. If you're not into kitsch and greasy spoons (especially if you're a nature-lover and the weather's good), skip Blackpool and spend more time in North Wales or the Lakes District. If you're not interested in an evening variety show or the night scene, give Blackpool a short midday stop and head into the Lakes District.

Transportation: Ruthin to Blackpool (100 miles)

Blackpool's the hot spot, and once you hit the motorway, you're a heat-seeking missile. From Ruthin, take A494 through the town of Mold and follow the blue signs to the motorway. M56 zips you to M6, where you'll turn north toward Preston and Lancaster. After Preston, take M55 into Blackpool and drive as close as you can to the stubby Eiffel-type tower in the town center. If you're not spending the day, head for a garage. If you're spending the night, drive to the waterfront and head north or south. All my recommended B&Bs are on the Promenade.

If you're using public transportation, get to Chester by bus. From Chester, it's 3-hour train ride to Blackpool, with transfers at Warrington Bank Quay and Preston (hourly).

Blackpool Orientation

Everything clusters along the 6-mile beachfront Promenade. Vintage trolley cars (70p a ride or £3.50 for a day-pass) run every few minutes, connecting everything on the waterfront. Parking downtown is terrible. Either stay at a B&B with parking or leave your car in one of the huge central garages (£6 a day). Each of the three amusement piers has its own personality (north—sedate, central—young fun, south—family, with a Wild West and circus theme). Stroll the promenade. A million greedy doors try every trick to get you inside. Huge arcade halls advertise free toilets and broadcast bingo numbers into the streets, the wind machine under a wax Marilyn Monroe blows at a steady gale, and the smell of fries, tobacco, and sugar is everywhere. Milk comes in raspberry or banana in this land where people under incredibly bad wigs look normal. Gypsy Rosalee-type spiritualists are a fix-

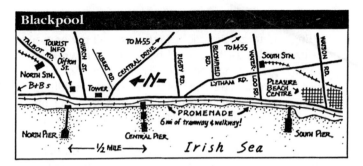

ture at Blackpool. I was told I mustn't leave without having my fortune told. But at £3 per palm, I'll read them myself.

Sightseeing Highlights

Tourist Information Office—First of all, go to the TI (9:00 a.m.-5:00 p.m., 10:00 a.m.-4:00 p.m. on Sunday, shorter hours off-season, tel. 0253/21623 or 26666 for 24-hour recorded entertainment information). Get the city map (35p), pick up brochures from all the amusement centers, and go over your plans. Ask about special shows and evening events.

▲Blackpool Tower—This vertical fun center is celebrating its 100th birthday in 1994. You pay about £7 to get in; after that, the fun is free. Work your way up from the bottom through layer after layer of noisy entertainment: circus, bug zone, space world, dinosaur land, aquarium, and the silly house of horrors. Have a coffee break in the very elegant ballroom with barely live music and golden oldies dancing to golden oldies all day. The finale, at the tip of this 500-foot-tall symbol of Blackpool, is a smashing view, especially at sunset (daily 10:00 a.m.-11:00 p.m.).

▲▲Variety Show—Blackpool always has a few razzle-dazzle music, dancing-girl, racy-humor, magic, and tumbling shows. Box offices around town can give you a rundown on what's available (tickets, £5 to £12). I enjoy the "old-time music hall shows." The shows are corny—neither hip nor polished—but it's fascinating to be surrounded by hundreds of partying British seniors, swooning again and waving their hankies to the predictable beat. Busloads of happy widows come from all corners of North England to giggle at jokes I'd never tell my grandma. **The Illuminations**—Blackpool was the first town in England to "go electric." Now, every September and October, Blackpool stretches its tourist season by illuminating its 6 miles of waterfront with countless lights, all blinking and twinkling, to the delight of those who visit this electronic festival. The American in me kept saying, "I've seen bigger and I've seen better," but I filled his mouth with cotton candy and just had some simple fun like everyone else on my specially decorated tram.

▲**Pleasure Beach**—These 42 acres of rides (more than 80, including "the best selection of white-knuckle rides in Europe"), ice-skating shows, cabarets, and amusements attract 6 million people a year. In 1994, it will open the "world's fastest and highest" roller coaster (235 feet, 85 mph). Admission is free, rides aren't (tel. 0253/341033). There are several other major amusement centers, including a popular water-park called Sand Castle.

▲▲▲**People-Watching**—Blackpool's top sight is its people. You'll see England here like nowhere else. Grab someone's hand and a big stick of "rock" (candy) and stroll. Ponder the thought of actually retiring here to spend your last years, day after day, surrounded by Blackpool and wearing a hat with a built-in ponytail.

Accommodations in Blackpool (£1 = about $1.50, tel. code: 0253)

Blackpool's 140,000 people provide 120,000 beds in 3,500 mostly dumpy, cheap, nondescript hotels and B&Bs. It's in the business of accommodating the English who can't afford to go to Spain. Almost all the B&Bs have the same design—minimal character, maximum number of springy beds—and charge £10 to £15 per person. Arriving midday, you should have no trouble finding a place. September to November and summer weekends are most crowded. My listings are all on the waterfront. View rooms seem to be a bit bigger (and cost no more), but suffer from a little trolley noise. The first three are in the quiet area, about a mile or two north of the Tower, with easy parking. The last is to the south, very close to the eye of the storm. All B&Bs charge a little more during the Illuminations. Prices may be soft in off-season.

The Robin Hood Hotel is a super place, cheery, family-run, with a big, welcoming living room and 12 newly and tastefully refurbished rooms with the only sturdy beds I found. (£20 per person, £18 for two-night stays, CC-VM, 1½ miles north of Tower across from a peaceful stretch of beach, 100 Queens Promenade, North Shore FY2 9NS, tel. 51599, Pam Webster.)

The Sheralea, a few doors down, is also family-run, new-ish, clean and cheery. (D-£28, DB-£32, springy beds, one family room with a bunk and a double; 86 Queens Promenade, tel. 57694, Ruth and Brian Catlow.)

The Prefect Hotel is all smiles and pink-flamingo pretty. (Divine would've loved it.) It's shabby but spacious-for-Blackpool with all the fun touches (S-£13, D-£26, DB-£28, 2 miles north of Tower at 204 Queens Promenade, FY2 9JS, tel. 52699, Bill and Pauline Acton).

The **Belmont Private Hotel**, right in the center, is not quite as terrible as its neighbors. Right on the waterfront, it's family-run with a decent meal service and a pleasant TV waterfront lounge (S-£14.50, D-£29, DB-£35, cheaper for two nights, springy beds; south of Tower between the central and south pier at 299 Promenade, Blackpool South, FY1 6AL, tel. 45815, Frank and Joan Linacre). The son, James, swears (believably) he'll eat your breakfast if you show up one minute after 9:00 a.m. The Pickwick Hotel (D-£26, DB-£32, 93 Albert Road, Blackpool FY1 4PW, tel. 24229), near the tower, off the water, is not as sleepable, but apparently good enough for the masses.

Itinerary Options

Many people love old Chester, and you'll drive right by it today. I'd skip it. It's a second-rate York.

Liverpool, a gritty but surprisingly enjoyable city, is a fascinating stop en route to Blackpool for Beatles fans and those who would like to look urban England straight in its problem-plagued, not-a-fairy-tale-in-sight eyes. (TI tel. 051/709-3631.) From Ruthin, get to the M53, which tun-

nels under the Mersey River. Once in town, follow the
signs to Pier Head and park just past the huge, curiously
named Royal Liver Building in the Maritime Museum car
park (easy, safe parking). The interesting Merseyside
Maritime Museum, cornerstone of a huge urban renewal
project, tells the story of this once-prosperous shipping
center—ships, immigrations, hard times, and good times
(£1.50). Nearby are plenty of lively shops, restaurants, and
the new Beatles Story (also at Albert Dock, an exhibition
that tells the whole rockin' story). Beatles fans will want to
explore Matthew Street a few blocks away, including the
famous, now-restored Cavern Club and the Beatles Shop
at #31. Next door, the Museum of Liverpool Life gives you
a look at the workaday story of the town. Another
Liverpool attraction is its people. Be sure to break the
conversational ice and get to know a Liverpudlian.
Leaving Liverpool, drive north along the waterfront following signs to M58, then M6, and finally M55 into the
day's second pool—Blackpool.

THE WINDERMERE LAKE DISTRICT

Blackpool to the Cumbrian Lake District is another study in contrast. After a 2-hour drive, you'll be in the heart of Wordsworth Country. If you were never a poet, here's your chance in a land where nature rules and man keeps a wide-eyed but low profile. Get oriented in the Lake District, enjoying a boat ride and the best 6-mile walk it has to offer, before setting up in the most remote and scenic accommodations of this trip.

Suggested Schedule

9:00	Breakfast (earlier if possible—unlikely in Blackpool).
9:30	Drive north
11:00	Visit Brockhole National Park Visitors Centre. See the orientation movie at 11:00, then get a map and guidebook, talk to the information staff, browse through exhibits, picnic on the grounds, play croquet, or lunch in the cafeteria.
1:00	Drive to Ullswater lake. Park at Glenridding.
1:45	Buy a boat ticket.
2:00	Catch the boat (departs 2:00 and 2:30).
2:35	Hike from Howtown to Glenridding.
6:00	Drive to your B&B.

Itinerary Options

If you can visit Wordsworth's Dove Cottage today, tomorrow will be even more relaxing. Consider a morning trip to Dove Cottage instead of Brockhole. Or if the weather's bad, do the cottage instead of the afternoon hike.

If great scenery is commonplace in your life, the Lake District can be more soothing (and wet) than exciting. To save time, you could easily make this area a one-night stand—or even a quick drive-through.

Transportation: Blackpool to Windermere (60 miles, 2 hours)

Drivers leave Blackpool taking M55 south to M6. Then zip north on M6. Exit on "A590/A591" through the towns of

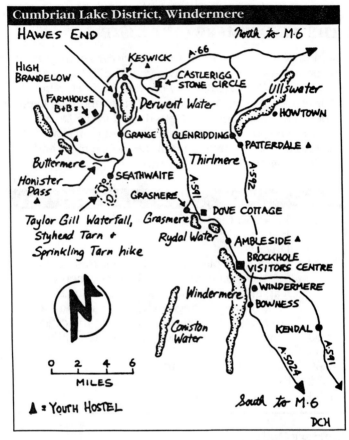

Cumbrian Lake District, Windermere

HAWES END

HIGH BRANDELOW

KESWICK   A·66

CASTLERIGG STONE CIRCLE

FARMHOUSE B+B's

Derwent Water

Ullswater

North to M·6

HOWTOWN

GRANGE   GLENRIDDING

PATTERDALE

Buttermere

Thirlmere

Honister Pass

SEATHWAITE

GRASMERE

A·591

DOVE COTTAGE

Taylor Gill Waterfall, Styhead Tarn + Sprinkling Tarn hike

Grasmere

Rydal Water

AMBLESIDE

A·592

BROCKHOLE VISITORS CENTRE

N

Windermere

WINDERMERE

BOWNESS

Coniston Water

KENDAL

0   2   4   6
MILES

A·5074   A·591

▲ = YOUTH HOSTEL

South to M·6

DCH

Kendal and Windermere to reach Brockhole National Park Visitors Centre. From Brockhole, take the tiny road northeast directly to Troutbeck. Then follow A592 to Glenridding and lovely Ullswater. Just before Glenridding, turn right into the car park and boat dock (get a self-service pay 'n' display parking sticker). Catch the 2:00 boat, sail for 35 minutes, get off at Howtown, and hike back to your car. Then drive north along the lake, turning left on A5091 and left again on A66 to Keswick. Your B&B is over Newlands Pass.

From Blackpool, train travelers will head to Penrith, with a transfer at Preston (1½ hours, hourly). Penrith is the nearest train station to the Lake District. The X5 Lakes

Link buses run between Penrith and Keswick (six buses daily between 8:34 a.m. and 5:00 p.m., except Sunday, 40-minute trip, tel. 0946/63222). While the Cumbrian Lake District is notorious for its frustrating public transportation schedule, a short visit without wheels is pretty easy if you keep it simple and focus only on the best (Keswick-area, Derwentwater). The Keswick bus station, good B&Bs, town center, TI office, bike rental place, Mountain Goat mini-bus tour starting point, and lake boat service are all within a 5-minute walk of each other. Numerous TI brochures lay out good hikes from Keswick with or without the help of local buses and boats.

Sightseeing Highlights

▲▲**Brockhole National Park Visitors Centre**—Start your visit to the Lake District here. Check the events board as you enter. The center offers a 17-minute intro-duction-to-the-lakes slide show at 11:00, an information desk, organized walks, exhibits, a book shop, a good cafeteria, gardens, nature walks, and a large car park. It's in a stately old lakeside mansion between Ambleside and the town of Windermere on A591 (daily 10:00 a.m.-6:00 p.m., until 5:00 in spring and fall, free entry but £2 to park, tel. 05394/46601). Consider buying a guidebook, the Ordnance Survey "Lake District Tourist Map" (£4.25), or possibly the more focused 1:25,000 OS Outdoor Leisure map for the northwest quarter of the area. I enjoyed the refreshingly opinionated *Good Guide to the Lakes* by Hunter Davies (£5). Go over your plans (such as the Ullswater ferry schedule) with the TI person.

The whole district is dotted with helpful Tourist Information Centres that are especially knowledgeable for their specific locality. Ask their advice. For the latest Lake District weather report, call 09662/45151.

▲▲▲**Ullswater Hike and Boat Ride**—Long narrow Ullswater, with 8 miles of diverse and grand Lake District scenery, is considered by many to be the most beautiful lake in the area. While you can drive it or cruise it, I'd ride the boat from the south tip halfway up and hike back. Park your car at the Glenridding dock. Boats leave

Glenridding regularly from 10:00 a.m. to 4:30 p.m. (2:00
and 2:30 departures, get there a little early in summer, 35-
minute ride, £2.50, tel. 07684/82229). Ride to the first stop,
Howtown, halfway up the lake. Then spend 4 hours hiking and dawdling along the well-marked path by the lake
south to Patterdale and then along the road back to your
car in Glenridding. This is a serious 6-mile walk with good
views, varied terrain, and a few bridges and farms along
the way. Wear good shoes and be prepared for rain. For a
shorter hike, consider a circular walk from Howtown Pier
(returning to catch a later boat back for no extra charge.)
There are several steamer trips daily up and down
Ullswater. A good rainy-day plan is to ride the covered
boat up and down the 8-mile lake (2 hours) or to
Howtown and back (1 hour). Novice pony-trekkers can
rent a pony at the Side Farm (just out of Patterdale, tel.
07684/82337) for a £6, hour-long scenic clip-clop above
the lake. More ambitious half-day rides are available.

▲**Beatrix Potter Sights**—Many come to the lakes on a
Beatrix Potter pilgrimage. Sensing that, entrepreneurial
locals have dreamed up a number of BP sights. It can be
confusing. Most important (and least advertised) is **Hill
Top Farm**, the seventeenth-century cottage where she
wrote many of her Peter Rabbit books (£3.20, April-
October 11:00 a.m.-5:00 p.m., closed Thursday and Friday,
next to Sawrey, near Hawkshead, tel. 05394/36269). Small,
dark and crowded, it gives a good look at her life and
work. (The nearby village of Hawkshead and the short
walk to the tiny lake, Tarn Hows, are both worth a stop.)
The Beatrix Potter Gallery shows off BP's original draw-
ings and watercolor illustrations used for her children's
storybooks, and tells more about her life and work (£2.40,
closed Saturday and Sunday, on Main Street in
Hawkshead, tel. 05394/36355). **The World of Beatrix
Potter**, a high-tech film and video tour into the world of
Mrs. Tiggy-winkle and company, is a hit with families and
the Japanese (£2.75, daily 10:00 a.m.-7:00 p.m., in
Bowness near Windermere town, tel. 05394/88444). And
up in the north, Keswick has gotten in on the BP action
with a **Beatrix Potter's Lake District** exhibit, little more

than a 16-minute National Trust video effort to remind us that BP was an environmentalist and we should be, too (£2.50, daily 10:00 a.m.-5:00 p.m., tel. 07687/75173).

Accommodations in and near Keswick (£1 = about $1.50, tel. code: 07687)

The Lake District abounds with attractive B&Bs, guest houses, and youth hostels. It needs them all when summer hordes threaten the serenity of this romantics' mecca. The region is most crowded on Sundays and in July and August. Saturdays (when people's week-long visits end) are not bad. With the mobility of a car, you should have no trouble finding a room. But to get a particular place, it's best to call ahead. Those on public transportation should stay in Keswick (first five listings). With a car, drive into a remote farmhouse experience (later listings). Those on a tight budget should take advantage of the area's fine youth hostels.

Berkeley Guest House, a big slate mansion on a quiet, elegant crescent between the bus station, the town, and the lakeside park, rubs drainpipes with fancier places. Enthusiastically run by Barbara Crompton, it has a pleasant lounge, cramped hallways and thoughtfully appointed, comfortable rooms. Request a view room. The chirpy but simple twin in the attic is a fine value if you don't mind the stairs (D-£29, DB-£37; The Heads, Keswick, Cumbria, CA12 5ER, tel. 74222).

The Highfield Hotel, next door, is good for those wanting the impersonality of a classy hotel with better public areas than rooms (S-£17, DB-£43, DB with big bay window lake views-£53; The Heads, tel. 72508).

Abacourt House, an old Victorian townhouse completely re-done by Sheila and Bill Newman, is on a quiet street lined with mostly dumpy B&Bs 2 blocks from the bus station and the town center. This non-smoking place is small, but clean and cheery, with a dark woody feeling. All four doubles have firm beds, TVs, and shiny modern bathrooms (DB-£38, £40 for one-nighters; 26 Stanger Street, Keswick, CA12 5JU, tel. 72967).

The Rowan Tree, another small, cheery, smoke-free place, a few doors down the street, has a few rooms without private facilities, making it less expensive and a fine budget value (D-£26, DB-£36; 18 Stanger Street, tel. 74304, Liz and Dave Thompson).

Ridgeway Guest House, on the top of the street, is a bit smoky and musty, but has decent beds and is just plain cheap (S-£11, D-£22; 25 Stanger Street, tel. 72582, Mrs. Hodgson).

Birkrigg Farm—This is the perfect farmhouse B&B for this trip. Mrs. Margaret Beaty offers visitors a comfy lounge, evening tea (good for socializing with her other guests), a classy breakfast, territorial view, perfect peace, and, upon request, a hot-water bottle to warm up your bed (traditionally, farmhouses lacked central heating). Her 220-acre working farm, shown on the Ordnance Survey map, is on a tiny road halfway between Braithwaite and Buttermere in the vast, majestic Newlands Valley. Leave Keswick heading west on the Cockermouth road (A68). Take the Newlands Valley exit and follow signs through Newlands Valley, direction Buttermere, a couple of miles until you see the B&B sign (£14 per person in S, D, T, or Q, family deals, one shared shower for six rooms, open April-November; Birkrigg Farm, Newlands Pass Rd., Keswick, Cumbria, CA12 5TS, tel. 78278).

Keskadale Farm B&B—Another great farmhouse experience with valley views and flapjack hospitality, this is a working farm with lots of curly-horned sheep and three rooms to rent (£14 per person in D or T, March-November, 2 minutes farther down Newlands Pass Road near a hairpin turn, Keskadale Farm, Newlands, Keswick CA12 5TS, tel. 78544, Margaret Harryman).

Since neither farmhouse serves dinner, take the lovely 10-minute drive to Buttermere for your evening meal at the **Fish Hotel pub** (£5, 6:00-9:00 nightly, limited menu, good fish, chips for vegetables) or the **Bridge Hotel pub** (£6 or £7, 6:00-9:30 nightly, more interesting menu and crowd).

For village B&Bs south of Derwentwater, try the beautiful Valley of Borrowdale. The tidy village of Grange has several neatly stacked slate B&Bs. The smaller stone-farm, mossy-roofed, cobbled village jumble of Rosthwaite is cow-dung basic. The Tolkienesque **Yew Tree Farm** (DB-£36, tel. 77675, Hazel Relph) and the less ancient, more spacious **Nook Farm** (D-£28, tel. 77677, Carole Jackson) are each comfortable but hearthocentric, with very old, sagging floors; thick, whitewashed walls; three rooms and small doorways. If you're under six feet tall and interested in farm noises and the Old World, these are for you.

Youth Hostels—The Lake District has thirty youth hostels and needs more. Most are in great old buildings, handy sources of information, fun socially, and inexpensive (£6 to £9 a bed). In the summer, you'll need to call ahead. For this plan, consider the **Buttermere King George VI Memorial Hostel**, a quarter-mile south of Buttermere village on Honister Pass Road (good food, family rooms, royal setting, tel. 70245), or the **Longthwaite Hostel**, secluded in Borrowdale Valley just south of Rosthwaite (well-run, drying rooms, tel. 77257). Two former hotels now operate as hostels: **Keswick** (center of town, tel. 72484) and **Derwentwater** (2 miles south of Keswick, tel. 77246).

EXPLORING THE LAKE DISTRICT

Fill today with your choice of great Lake District walks and a visit to the humble house of William Wordsworth, the poet whose appreciation of nature and back-to-basics lifestyle put this area on the map. If you need a vacation from your vacation, use this day to just vegetate and recharge. The sky will cloud and clear. You'll probably have rain mixed with brilliant bright spells. Handy pubs offer atmospheric shelter at every turn.

Suggested Schedule	
9:00	Slow breakfast, enjoy your farm.
10:00	Explore Buttermere Lake and drive over Honister Pass.
1:00	Tour Wordsworth's Dove Cottage and museum.
12:00	Drive to Warwick, picnic at the castle.
1:00	Tour the Warwick castle.
3:00	Explore the lake called Derwentwater. See the town of Keswick, cruise to High Brandlehow Pier. Hike up to Cat Bells (or along lake) and down to Hawes End Pier (or vice versa). Catch the boat back to Keswick. (If the weather's good, do this hike in the morning.)
6:00	Drive home.

Transportation around Keswick and Derwentwater

By car, nothing is very far from Keswick and Derwent-water. The entire region is just 30 miles by 30 miles. Get a good map, get off the big roads, and leave the car, at least occasionally, for some walking. In the summer, the Keswick-Ambleside-Windermere-Bowness area suffers from congestion.

Those without wheels should take advantage of several publications (from the TI or in most B&B libraries), especially *Explore Lakeland and Cumbria: Out and About From Keswick* (which details the best hikes from Keswick, taking advantage of one-way bus connections) and *15 Walks From Keswick* (£1.95). Mountain Goat Tours run all-day

(£20) and half-day (£10) mini-bus tours daily from Keswick. They are rugged, informative (led by established mountain guides), and great for people who'd like to see the area without hiking and don't have a car. Unfortunately, you may not know if your tour will reach its minimum number of six passengers until shortly before departure (office at Keswick central car park, tel. 73962).

Sightseeing Highlights—on or near Derwentwater

▲**Keswick**—As far as touristy lake district centers go, Keswick is an enjoyable town (population: 5,000). For our plans, this is your logistical headquarters with everything you need (easy bus to Penrith and England's train system, good regional TI, several mediocre but entertaining museums, bus tours, a suburb called Barf, and plenty of good B&Bs). It's situated right on the best single lake in the area for our visit, Derwentwater. Keswick's market square, central car park, lakeside boat landing, TI, and recommended B&Bs are all within a 5-minute walk of each other (TI, Market Square, tel. 07687/72645).

▲▲**Derwentwater** is one of the region's most photographed and popular lakes. With four islands, good circular boat service, plenty of trails, and the pleasant town of Keswick at its north end, the lake entertains.

The roadside views aren't much, so walk or cruise. You can walk around the lake (fine trail, but floods in heavy rains, 9 miles, 3 hours), cruise it (50 minutes), or do a hike/sail mix. I suggest a hike/sail trip around the lake. Boats run about every 30 minutes in each direction and make seven stops on each 50-minute round-trip. The best hour-long lakeside walk is between the docks at High Brandlehow and Hawse End. (The boat trip costs £4.25 per circle with free stop-overs, or 60p per segment. Stand on the pier or the boat may not stop.)

▲▲**Cat Bells High Ridge Hike**—For a great "king of the mountain" feeling, great all-around views, and a close-up look at the weather blowing over the ridge, hike about 2 hours from Hawse End up along the ridge to Cat Bells (1,480 feet), and down to High Brandlehow. From there you can catch the boat, or take the easy path along the shore of Derwentwater to your Hawes End starting point. This is probably the most dramatic family walk in the area. For a longer and higher hike, continue farther along the ridge to Black Crag, and walk down to Grange or High Brandlehow. Warning: Every year, careless hikers underestimate the need for sturdy shoes, raingear, and maps. This lush world is not as gentle as it looks. Get specific hiking advice from a tourist center. There's a not-particularly-safe little car park at Hawes End. From Keswick, the lake, or your farmhouse B&B, you can see silhouetted stick figures hiking along this ridge.

▲▲**A Waterfall and Two Tarns Hike**—For a more difficult and equally rewarding 3-hour Derwentwater-area hike, park south of Borrowdale, at the end of the long dead-end road to Seathwaite. Go through the farm, cross the river, continue along the river (it's difficult to follow the trail; stay near the river) and up a steep, rocky climb to the Taylor Gill Force, a 140-foot waterfall. There's a tough hundred yards of rocky scramble, but the trail improves at the falls. Keep walking to two sleeping-beauty tarns (bodies of water too small to be lakes, Styhead and Sprinkling Tarn), circle the Seathwaite Fell to Stockley Bridge, and follow the bridle-path back to your car. For an easier version, just hike to the first tarn and backtrack, eventually taking a right turn leading to Stockley Bridge (get specifics on this hike from the TI).

▲▲**Buttermere**—This ideal little lake with a lovely encircling 4-mile stroll offers non-stop, no-sweat, lakeland beauty. If you're not a hiker, but kind of wish you were, take this walk. If you're very short on time, at least stop here and get your shoes dirty. (Parking and pubs in Buttermere village.) A great road over the rugged Honister Pass, strewn with nosy ragamuffin goats and glacial debris, connects Buttermere with Borrowdale and Derwentwater.

▲**Castlerigg Stone Circle**—These 38 stones, 90 feet across, 3,000 years old, are mysteriously laid out on a line between the two tallest peaks on the horizon. For maximum goosebumps, be here at sunrise or sunset (free, open all the time, follow brown signs as you head east from Keswick, 3 minutes off A66, easy parking).

Other Lake District Sights:

▲▲Dove Cottage—Wordsworth spent his most productive years (1799-1808) in this well-preserved old cottage on the edge of Grasmere. Today it's the obligatory sight for any Lake District visit. Even if you're not a fan, Wordsworth's "plain living and high thinking," his appreciation of nature, his romanticism, and the ways his friends unleashed their creative talents are very appealing. The cottage tour and adjoining museum are excellent. Even a speedy, jaded museum-goer will want at least an hour here (£3.80, daily 9:30 a.m.-5:30 p.m., tel. 05394/35544.)

Rydal Mount—Wordsworth's final, higher-class home with a lovely garden and view lacks the charm of Dove Cottage. It's worthwhile only for Wordsworth fans.

Hard Knott Pass—Only 1,300 feet above sea level, this pass is a thriller, with a narrow, winding, steeply graded road. Just over the pass are the scant, but evocative, remains of the Hard Knott Roman Fortress. Great views, miserable rainstorms, frustrating and very slow when the one-lane road with turn-outs is clogged by traffic.

Helvellyn—Often considered the best high-mountain hike in Cumbria, this dangerous, breathtaking, round-trip hike from Glenridding has a glorious ridge-walk finale. Be careful, do this 4-hour hike only in good weather, and get advice from the Glenridding tourist office. Stupendous views, but keep one eye on the trail.

Sellafield Nuclear Power Plant—This leading British nuclear site once had a reputation so bad it had to change its name. It now gives classy free tours, wowing visitors with the wonders of nuclear power, an odd way to brighten a grey day (west of the lakes, on the coast, 45 minutes from Keswick or Hard Knott Pass, daily 10:00 a.m.-6:00 p.m., until 4:00 p.m. in winter, free 40-minute bus tours of the grounds followed by an exhibit, departures about every half-hour, tel. 09467/27027).

THE LAKE DISTRICT TO THE WEST OF SCOTLAND

Today you'll drive for 6 hours to Oban, a gateway to the Hebrides, Scotland's wild and windblown western islands. The last half of the journey is scenic, taking you from big, burly Glasgow, along the famous Loch Lomond, deep into the powerful mountains, forests, valleys, and lochs of Scotland's west country, and to the edge of the Highlands.

Suggested Schedule

9:00	Short stop at the Castlerigg stone circle before leaving the Lake District.
1:00	Lunch on Loch Lomond. Drive on, stopping at Inveraray, enjoying the rugged scenery en route.
4:00	Arrive in Oban. Park near train station, tour the whiskey distillery, drop by the tourist office.
8:30	Have dinner and music at McTavish's Kitchen.

Transportation: Lake District to Oban (220 miles)
From Keswick, take A66 18 miles to M6 and speed non-stop north (via Penrith and Carlisle), crossing Hadrian's Wall into bonnie Scotland. The road stays great, becoming the M74 south of Glasgow. To slip quickly through Glasgow, leave M74 at junction 4 onto M73, following signs to M8/Glasgow. Leave M73 at junction 2, exiting onto M8. Stay on M8 west through Glasgow, exiting on junction 30, cross the Erskine Bridge (60p), and turn left on A82, following signs to Crianlarich. (For a scenic drive through Glasgow, take exit 17 off M8 and stay on A82, direction Dumbarton.) In a few minutes you'll be driving along scenic Loch Lomond. The first picnic turnout has the best lake views, lots of benches, a grassy park and kids' playground.

Halfway up the loch, at Tarbet, take the "tourist route" left onto A83, drive along saltwater Loch Long and toward Inveraray via Rest-and-Be-Thankful Pass. (This colorful name comes from the 1880s, when second- and third-class

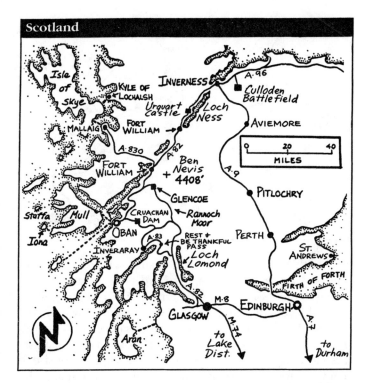

coach passengers got out and pushed the coach and first-class passengers up the hill.)

Inveraray is a lovely castle town on Loch Fyne. Park near the pier. How's the fishing? The town jail is an entertaining "nineteenth-century living prison" museum (£3.60, daily 9:30 a.m.-6:00 p.m., tel. 0499/2381). Leaving Inveraray, drive through a gate (at the Woolen Mill) to A819, through Glen Aray and along scenic Loch Awe where A85 takes you into Oban.

If you're using public transportation, take the bus from Keswick to Penrith (40 minutes, six daily), catch a train to Glasgow (2 hours, nine daily) and transfer to a train to Oban (3 hours, four daily).

Oban

Oban, called the "gateway to the isles," is a busy little ferry and train terminal with a charming shiver-and-bustle

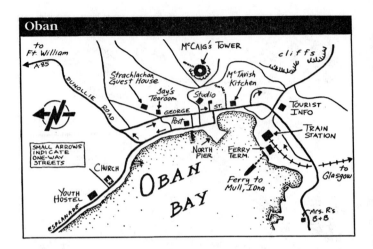

vitality that gives you a feel for small-town Scotland. The
business action, just a couple of streets deep, stretches
along the harbor and its promenade. Wind, boats, gulls,
several layers of islands, and the promise of a wide-open
Atlantic beyond, give it a rugged and salty charm. There's
nothing earth-shaking to see. But parking is easy, sights
are close together, and the town seems eager to please its
many visitors. There's live, fairly touristy music nightly in
several bars and restaurants, shops sell woolen and tweed
with cash registers cocked (open until 8:00 p.m. and on
Sunday), and posters announce a variety of enticing island
day tours. The unfinished "colosseum" on the hill overlooking the town (McCaig's Tower, 1897) was an "employ
the workers and build me a fine memorial" project under-
taken by an early Oban tycoon.

The TI has brochures listing everything from saunas to
launderettes to horse-riding to rainy-day activities, and a
fine bookshop (Monday-Saturday, 9:00 a.m.-8:45 p.m.,
Sunday 10:00 a.m.-5:00 p.m., shorter hours outside of July
and August, tel. 0631/63122).

Sightseeing Highlights in and around Oban

Oban Experience—This wimpy exhibit offers a little his-
tory-of-Oban slideshow, followed by a 30-minute Skye
High BBC show helicoptering you around the wondrous

Isle of Skye. It's a good way to spend 45 minutes if you have a partner shopping in the giant Heritage Wharf woolen shop next door (£1, daily 9:00 a.m.-5:00 p.m. and summer Sundays 10:30 a.m.-5:00 p.m., at the ferry terminal, next to the train station, free glass-blowing demonstration next door, tel. 66969).

▲**West Highland Malt Scotch Whiskey Distillery Tours**—The Oban whiskey distillery, celebrating its 200th birthday in 1994, produces 14,000 liters a week. They offer serious and fragrant 40-minute, £2 tours explaining the process from start to finish, with a free, smooth sample in the middle and a discount coupon for the shop at the end. The free exhibition preceding the tour gives a quick history of Scotland and its whiskey. This is the handiest whiskey tour on our route, just a block off the harbor (Monday-Friday and in-season Saturdays, 9:30 a.m.-5:00 p.m., last tour at 4:15, to avoid a very long wait, call to reserve a place, tel. 64262).

Tour Iona and Mull—For the best 1-day look at the dramatic and historic island scenery around Oban, take one of several Iona/Mull tours offered in Oban. The Isle of Mull, the third largest in Scotland, has 300 scenic miles of coastline, a castle, and a 3,169-foot-high mountain. The stark, historic, and car-free island of Iona is connected to the western tip of Mull by a tiny regular ferry. St. Columba brought Christianity to Scotland via the Iona Abbey in A.D. 590. Near the abbey is a thirteenth-century Benedictine nunnery, a burial place of ancient kings, an ecumenical community, a museum, and a few shops, pubs, and B&Bs.

The island tours include the Oban-Mull ferry (60 minutes), an entertaining and informative bus ride across the Isle of Mull (90 minutes), the small ferry connection to Iona (20 minutes), time to roam on Iona (2 hours), and a return to Oban via ferry (£14 on Bowman's, 10:00 a.m.-5:30 p.m., best in fair weather, tel. 63221). Schedules are flexible if you want more time in Mull or an extension to the wildly scenic Isle of Staffa with Fingal's Cave. Guides are local boys who know how to spin a yarn, making historical trivia fascinating, or at least fun. There are several tours and companies to choose from. Taking your car onto the ferry is very expensive (£20 each way).

Two quick, easy opportunities to get that romantic island experience: Explore the stark but very green island of Kerrera, just opposite Oban (£2 round-trip, upon request, at Gallanach's dock, 2 miles south of Oban). Drive 15 miles south of Oban to the Isle of Seil, connected to the mainland by a bridge (see Eating, below). Enjoy a walk, solitude, and the sea.

Accommodations in Oban (£1 = about $1.50, tel. code: 0631)

Strathlachlan Guest House—This is a winner. Mrs. Rena Anderson's place is stocking-feet cozy, crackerjack friendly, and chocolate-box tidy. It's a spacious, uncluttered place with six rooms, solid beds, a great TV lounge, easy parking, and a good central location 2 blocks off the water just past Jay's Tearoom, 5 minutes' walk from the train station (S-£15, D-£30, T-£45, Q-£60, family deals; 2 Strathaven Terrace, Oban, Argyll, tel. 63861).

Tanglin B&B, next door, is another fine value. Liz and Jim Montgomery offer a bright and brand-new-feeling place with springy beds, TVs in the rooms, and an easy-going atmosphere (S-£13, D-£26, DB-£32, ask about off-season rates and family deals on larger rooms; 3 Strathaven Terrace, tel. 63247). **The Raniven Guest House** (DB-£35, some non-smoking rooms; Strathlachlan Terrace, tel. 62713) and the **MacColl's B&B** (S-£15, D-£30, firm beds, noisy street; around the corner on Dunollie Road, tel. 65361) are sleepable.

The Barriemore Hotel is the last place (and only good value) on Oban's grand waterfront "Esplanade." It's a bit smoky, but has a classy dark, woody, equestrian feel with 15 spacious and comfortable rooms furnished like living rooms (DB-£40 to £52, CC-VM, firm beds, grand views, some easy-access ground floor rooms; The Esplanade, PA34 5AQ, tel. 66356, Evelyn and Jim McLean).

The **youth hostel**, on the Esplanade alongside the finest hotels in town, is in a grand building with a smashing harbor/island view (£7.50 per bed with sheets, nonmembers of any age welcome for £1.50 extra, 4- to 16-bed rooms, great facilities and public rooms, closed November-January, tel. 62025). Just a block from the TI and train station, and normally filled with backpackers in summer, is the **Jeremy Inglis B&B** (£7 per bed in basic, shared rooms with a continental breakfast; 21 Airds Crescent, Oban, tel. 65065 or 63064).

Just south of town, **Mrs. Robertson's B&B** is a mini-estate in a lush garden with a commanding view of the bay and islands. She rents a twin and a double (DB-£35; Dungrianach, Pulpit Hill, Oban, Argyll, PA34 4LX, tel. 62840). From the TI, go up Albany Street and take the second right up Pulpit Hill. When the road levels in a forest, turn right at the Dungrianach sign a half-block before a telephone booth.

Eating (with swirling kilts) in Oban

To mix a folk show inexpensively with dinner, eat at **McTavish's Kitchen**. Facing the harbor on central George Street, this huge eating hall (non-smokers get the best harbor views) is an Oban institution, featuring live, but tired, folk music and dancing nightly (mid-May through September). This is your basic tourist trap (as is virtually anything so traditionally Scottish), filled mostly with English vacationers. The food is inexpensive and edible (£5 for a basic plate, £13 for the super Scottish multi-course menu). The piping, dancing, and singing happens nightly from 8:30 to 10:30 (the three-person band plays two hour-long cycles, so you'll cover all the cultural bases in an hour). The show costs £3 without a meal, £1.50 with dinner, or free with dinner with a coupon from your B&B. No reservations required.

Jay's Tearoom, near my recommended B&Bs on George Street, is an elegant pastel teahouse humid with happy eaters. Open nightly until 10:00, it's a good place to try the Scottish equivalent of rice and beans: "haggis, tatties and neeps." (Haggis, my waitress admitted, is on the menu just for tourists. Like most young Scots, she had never tried it.)

The Studio is a small candle-lit restaurant featuring serious first-class Scottish cooking (£11 for a full Scottish meal, 5:00-10:00 nightly, tel. 0631/62030). It has a real hit-the-spot-on-a-stormy-day prawn-and-clam chowder and great trout.

For an interesting drive and dinner, head south from Oban on A816 to B844. Just over the bridge, on the Isle of Seil, is a pub called **Tigh-an-Truish** ("house of trousers"). After a 1745 English law forbid kilts on the mainland, Highlanders used this pub to change from kilts to trousers before crossing the bridge. The Tigh-an-Truish pub serves great meals to those in kilts or pants (meals daily, noon-2:15 p.m., 6:00-8:30 p.m., darts anytime, good seafood dish, crispy vegetables, tel. 08523/242). Five miles across the island is Easdale, a historic, touristy, windy, little slate-mining town facing the open Atlantic (tiny shuttle ferry to tiny island, tiny slate-town museum, incredibly tacky ego-maniac's "Highland Arts" shop).

Scottish Words
aye—yes
ben—mountain
bonnie—beautiful
carn—heap of stones
creag—rock, cliff
haggis—rich assortment of oats and sheep organs stuffed into a chunk of sheep intestine, liberally seasoned, boiled and eaten—mostly by tourists. Tastier than it sounds.
inch, innis—island
inver—river, mouth
kyle—strait, firth
loch—lake
neeps—turnips
tattie—potato

HIGHLANDS, LOCH NESS, SCENIC DRIVE

Today is mostly a scenic drive, your chance to see the harsh Highland beauty of Glencoe, the engineering beauty of the Caledonian Canal, and the mysterious beauty of Loch Ness—scenic even if you don't believe in the monster. How far you get today depends on the weather, the traffic, and your eagerness to get to bonnie Edinburgh.

Suggested Schedule	
9:00	Leave Oban.
10:00	Explore the valley of Glencoe, still weeping after the bloody clan massacre.
11:00	Drive from Glencoe to Fort Augustus.
12:00	Continue across Scotland, following the Caledonian Canal. Stop at Loch Ness to explore the castle and take care of monster business.
3:00	Visit the evocative Culloden Battlefield, near Inverness.
4:00	Drive south.
7:00	Set up in Edinburgh.

Itinerary Option
For a scenic short-cut, head north only as far as Glencoe (Loch Ness is not much to see), then cut over to Edinburgh via Rannoch Moor and Tyndrum. Many find Glencoe more interesting for an overnight than Oban.

Transportation: Oban to Glencoe (45 miles) to Loch Ness (75 miles) to Inverness (20 miles) to Edinburgh (150 miles)
You'll make great time on good, mostly two-lane roads today unless traffic gets in the way. Americans are generally timid about passing. Study the British. Be careful, but if you don't pass, diesel fumes and large trucks might be your memory of Day 16.

From Oban, follow the coastal A828 toward Fort William. At Loch Leven and Ballachulish village, leave A828, taking A82 into Glencoe. Drive through the village

into the valley for 10 minutes for a grand view of the vast
Rannoch Moor. Then make a U-turn and return through
the valley. Continue north on A82, over the bridge, past
Fort William toward Loch Ness. Scotland is sliced in half
by a series of lakes and canals known as the Caledonian
Canal. Follow the Caledonian Canal on A82 for 60 miles,
stopping at Loch Ness, then continuing on A82 to
Inverness.

Leaving Inverness, follow signs to A9 (south, direction:
Perth). Just as you leave Inverness, detour 4 miles east off
A9 on B9006 to visit the Culloden Battlefield Visitors
Centre. Back on A9, it's a wonderfully speedy and very
scenic highway (A9, M90, A90) all the way to Edinburgh.
If traffic is light and your foot is heavy, you can drive from
Inverness to Edinburgh in 3 hours. (For arrival in
Edinburgh, see Transportation section, Day 17.)

Six buses a day run from Oban to Inverness, through
Fort William (4 hours). Ask at the station for the exact
schedule and stops, so you can visit sites along the way,
catching a later bus as you go. Nine trains a day connect
Inverness, Pitlochry and Edinburgh (3½ hours).

Sightseeing Highlights between Oban and Edinburgh
▲▲**Glencoe** is the essence of the wild, powerful, and
stark beauty of the Highlands (and, I think, excuses the
hurried tourist from needing to go north of Inverness).
Along with its scenery, Glencoe offers a good dose of
bloody clan history. The visitors centre has a fine exhibit
with a 14-minute video about the massacre (30p, daily
9:30 a.m.-5:30 p.m., shorter hours or closed off-season,
just east of town on A82, tel. 08552/307). It tells about the
"murder under trust" of 1692, when the Campbells massa-
cred the sleeping MacDonalds and the valley got its nickname, "The Weeping Glen." For a good 1-mile walk, hike
to the Devil's Staircase (trail leaves from A82, 8 miles east
of Glencoe). For a 3-hour hike, ask at the visitors center
about walking to the "Lost Valley of the MacDonalds"
(trail leaves from A82, 3 miles east of Glencoe). For good
pub food in the glen, try the King's Hotel on A82.

In Glencoe village, Arthur Smith runs the **Cala Sona** B&B. Aptly named "house of happiness" in Gaelic, he entertains his guests with a peat fire, ghost stories, and tales of the Glencoe massacre (S-£12, D-£24, on the main street, tel. 08552/314). Nearest TI is in Ballachulish (tel. 08552/296).

Ben Nevis—At Fort William, you'll pass Ben Nevis, Great Britain's highest peak (more than 4,400 feet). Thousands of visitors walk to its summit each year, but just hope for a clear day and admire her from the car. Britain's only mountain cable-cars can take you to the not-very-lofty 2,150 foot level (signposted on A82, 12-minute ride, tel. 0397/705825).

▲**Caledonian Canal**—Three lochs and a series of canals cut Scotland in two. Oich, Lochy, and Ness were connected in the early 1800s by the great British engineer, Telford. As you drive the 60 miles from Fort William to Inverness, follow Telford's work—20 miles of canals and locks between 40 miles of lakes, raising ships from sea level to 51 feet (Ness) to 93 feet (Lochy) to 106 feet (Oich). For a good look at the locks, see "Neptune's Staircase" where you'll find a park built along a series of about ten locks (2 miles north of Fort William, detour 1 mile on A830). Fort Augustus is another good lock stop.

▲**Loch Ness**—I'll admit, I had my zoom lens out and my eyes on the water. The local tourist industry thrives on the legend of the Loch Ness monster. It's a thrilling thought, and there have been several seemingly reliable "sightings" (monks, policemen, and now sonar images). The Loch, 24 miles long, less than a mile wide, and the third deepest in Europe, is deepest near the Urquhart Castle. Most monster sightings are in this area.

The Nessie commercialization is so tacky that there are two "official" Loch Ness Exhibition Centres within 100 yards of each other. Each has a tour-bus parking lot and more square footage devoted to their shop than their exhibit. The first one (£3.50, daily 9:00 a.m.-8:30 p.m.) is a high-school-quality photo report followed by the 30-minute "We believe in the Loch Ness monster" movie, featuring credible-sounding locals explaining what they saw and a review of modern Nessie searches. The place closest to Inverness (in a big stone mansion) is a little better, with a 40-minute series of video bits on the geological and historical environment that bred the monster story and the various searches (£4, 9:00 a.m.-8:30 p.m.). The exhibits are fascinating, but way overpriced. The nearby Urquhart Castle ruins (£2, 9:30 a.m.-6:00 p.m.) are gloriously situated with a view of virtually the entire Loch Ness and, except for the crowds and parking problems, make for a better stop than either official monster center.

Inverness—The only sizable town in the north of Scotland, with 42,000 people, Inverness is pleasantly located on a river at the base of a castle (not worth a look) with a free little museum (worth a look, cheap café), a Highland Music museum (Balnain House, Tuesday-Sunday 10:00 a.m.-5:00 p.m., tracing the local music from heroic warrior songs to Gaelic rock, tel. 0463/715757), a bustling pedestrian downtown, and a good train connection to Edinburgh and London (TI tel. 0463/234353; for accommodations, see below).

▲**Culloden Battlefield**—Scottish troops under Bonnie Prince Charlie were defeated here in 1746 by the English. This last land battle fought on British soil spelled the end of Jacobite resistance and the fall of the clans. The visitors center makes the short detour worthwhile with a great exhibit, stirring 16-minute audiovisual show, a furnished old cottage, and the memorial battlegrounds (£1.50, daily 9:30 a.m.-6:00 p.m., shorter hours off-season, good tea room, tel. 0463/790607).

Pitlochry—This pleasant tourist town makes a pleasant overnight stop. Its Edradour Scotch distillery offers a free guided tour, audiovisual show, and of course, tasting (9:30 a.m.-5:00 p.m., closed Sunday, 2 miles east of town, tel. 0796/472095). The Blair Athol Distillery (half a mile from town, tel. 472234) gives £2 tours. Pitlochry also has a salmon ladder (jumping May and June, free viewing area, 10-minute walk from town) and plenty of forest walks. The town theater offers a different play every night. (TI, 9:00 a.m.-8:00 p.m., tel. 0796/472215, accommodations listed below.)

Accommodations in Inverness and Pitlochry

Here's where things get murky. You can get to Edinburgh if you really push. You'll arrive late, so be sure to have a firm hold on a bed and call at 5:00 p.m. with your estimated time of arrival (see Accommodations, Day 17). A more relaxed plan is to find a room in Inverness (3 hours from Edinburgh) or Pitlochry (1 hour from Edinburgh).

Inverness: These rooms are all a short walk from the train station and town center. The first two are on a quiet street just up the steps from the pedestrian High Street. **Ardconnel House** is tasteful, bright, spacious, and thoroughly classy (S-£16, D-£32, T-£48, family deals, TVs in rooms; 21 Ardconnel Street, IV2 3EU, tel. 0463/240455, Mrs. MacKenzie). **The Holies** is much simpler, but still a fine value, with only three rooms and sturdy beds (S-£13, D-£26, T-£39, family deals; 24 Ardconnel Street, tel. 0463/231291, Mrs. Proudfoot). The town **youth hostel** (up the street from the castle at 1 Old Edinburgh Road, tel. 0463/231771, 6- to 20-bed rooms) and the much more laid-back **Inverness Student Hotel** (£8 per bed with sheets in one of its ten 6-bed rooms, across the street from the hostel at 8 Culduthel Road, tel. 0463/236556) are cheap and central.

Pitlochry: Craigroyston House is ideal. It's a big Victorian country house with eight Laura Ashley-style rooms, piano in the lounge, just up the steps from the TI and run by charming Gretta Maxwell (£16 to £21 per person, all rooms with private bath, next to the church at 2 Lower Oakfield, PH16 5HQ, tel. 0796/472053). Mrs. Maxwell can find you another B&B if her place is full. Pitlochry's fine youth hostel is on Knockard Road above the main street (tel. 0796/472308).

EDINBURGH

Edinburgh is Scotland's showpiece. Historical, monumental, entertaining, and well-organized, it's a tourist's delight—one of Europe's great cities. Even if you don't go farther north, make time for Edinburgh (a 2-hour drive from the Lake District). While the major sights can be seen in a day, most visitors enjoy taking two days to explore the medieval town and Georgian town, and to browse in Scotland's most visit-worthy and entertaining city.

Suggested Schedule Day 17	
9:00	Drop off laundry.
10:00	Guided tour of Edinburgh Castle.
1:00	Lunch in Deacon Brodie's Pub.
2:00	Catch Royal Mile walking tour (or do it yourself).
4:00	Tour Holyrood Palace.
8:00	Evening show, pub or haunted walk (at 7:00 or 9:00).

Suggested Schedule Day 18	
9:00	Climb Sir Walter Scott Memorial for city view.
10:00	Visit the Georgian House, tour Georgian town.
1:00	More Royal Mile museum-going, shopping, tour the National Gallery, or take the "City, Sea, and Hills" bus tour.

Transportation
You'll be arriving late on Day 16 (or possibly at noon on Day 17, if you take more time in the north). Signs to "city centre" lead to the black, towering neo-Gothic Scott Memorial (near the castle). From there, drive down Princes Street, turn right over the North Bridge and follow the A68/Jedburgh signs to my recommended B&B's, all just beyond the big flat white Royal Commonwealth Pool building on Dalkeith Road. (Most are either on the first left or second right off Dalkeith Road after the pool.)

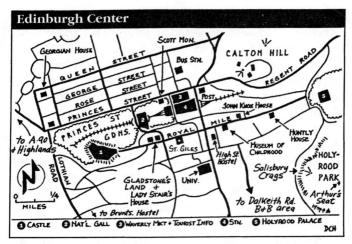

You won't need your car again until you leave Edinburgh. City buses (LRT information office at the corner of Waverley Bridge and Market Street, average fare 55p, tell the driver where you're going, drop exact change into box and grab your ticket as you board) and taxis (easy to flag down, several handy pick-up points, 90p drop charge, average ride between downtown and B&B district—£2.50) are easy and inexpensive, whereas parking and traffic are a real headache. Nearly all Edinburgh sights are within walking distance.

Arriving by train puts you in the city center a few steps from the TI and bus to B&Bs (catch Dalkeith Road buses from Princes Street on the C&A department store side of the street a block from the station, 50p, 7 minutes).

Orientation

Edinburgh (pronounced: ed'n-burah) is two towns divided by what was once a lake. The drained lake (Nor Loch) is now a lovely park and Waverley Bridge where you'll find the TI, Waverley Shopping Center/Food Court, train station, the starting point for most city bus tours, Tattoo/bus info office, festival office, the National Gallery, and a covered dance and music pavilion.

The old town grew along a volcanic ridge running south of the lake. Historic, fascinating buildings pack the Royal

Mile between castle (on the top) and Holyrood Palace (on the bottom). Houses, shops and arcades are tall and shoulder-to-shoulder, with "closes" (public lanes branching off into peaceful little courtyards) connected to High Street by narrow lanes or even tunnels. This colorful jumble, in its day the most crowded city in the world, is the tourist's Edinburgh and a great downhill walk.

To alleviate crowding, the lake was drained, and a magnificent Georgian city, today's New Town, was laid out to the north. Georgian Edinburgh, like Bath, shines with broad boulevards, straight streets, square squares, circular circuses, and elegant mansions decked out in colonnades, pediments, and sphinxes in the proud, neo-Classical style of 200 years ago.

The crowded tourist office, as central as can be atop the Waverley Market on Princes Street (9:00 a.m.-8:00 p.m., Sunday 11:00-8:00, shorter hours and closed Sunday in off-season, tel. 031/557-1700, best town map, well-worth £1), may not be worth the time in line. If the line's long, browse through the many free brochures in the racks, and consider buying the misnamed *Essential Guide to Edinburgh* (£1.50) and *The List*, the best monthly entertainment listing.

Sightseeing Highlights along the Royal Mile (in walking order from top to bottom)

▲▲▲Royal Mile—This is one of Europe's most interesting historic walks, whether you follow a local guide (daily at 11:00 a.m. and 2:00 p.m., often free during the festival, £3 other times, see below) or do it yourself with a Royal Mile guidebook. Each step of the way is entertaining. Start at the top and loiter down to the palace. I've listed the top sights of the Royal Mile—working downhill.

The Royal Mile is actually a series of different streets in a straight line. All along, you'll find interesting shops, cafés, and closes, providing the thoughtful visitor a few little rough edges of the old town. See it now. In a few years, it will be a string of tourist gimmicks, woolen shops, and contrived "sights."

▲▲Edinburgh Castle—The fortified birthplace of the city 1,300 years ago, this is the imposing symbol of

Edinburgh. Start with the free 20-minute guided introduction tour, which starts every few minutes from inside the gate. (See the clock for the next tour.) Don't miss the Scottish National War Memorial, the Banqueting Hall with fine Scottish Crown Jewels, the room full of Battle of Culloden mementos, St. Margaret's Chapel (oldest building in town), the giant cannon, and the city view from the ramparts (best seen in that order). Allow 90 minutes, including the tour. (£4, 9:30 a.m.-6:00 p.m., until 5:00 p.m. in winter and on holidays, tel. 244-3101.)

The Scotch Whiskey Heritage Centre is only for the desperate. Even with little whiskey kegs for train cars and toilets that actually got the "Loo of the Year" award, the Whiskey ride is a rip-off designed to distill £4 out of your pocket. **The Camera Obscura** across the street is also worth a miss.

▲▲**Gladstone's Land**—Take a good look at this typical sixteenth- to seventeenth-century house, complete with lived-in furnished interior and guides in each room who love to talk. (£2.40, April-October, 10:00 a.m.-5:00 p.m., Sunday 2:00-5:00 p.m., good Royal Mile photo from the top floor window or from the top of its entry stairway through the golden eagle.)

▲**Lady Stair's House**—This interesting house, which dates back to 1622, is filled with manuscripts and knickknacks of Scotland's three greatest literary figures: Robert Burns, Sir Walter Scott, and Robert Louis Stevenson. Interesting for anyone, orgasmic for fans (free, 10:00 a.m.-6:00 p.m., till 5:00 p.m. off-season, closed Sunday).

▲**St. Giles Cathedral**—Don't miss this engaging Gothic church's ornate, medieval thistle chapel (to the right of the altar, 50p) or the Scottish crown steeple on top (daily 9:00 a.m.-7:00 p.m., until 5:00 p.m. off-season, fine café downstairs). John Knox, founder of austere Scottish Presbyterianism, is buried, austerely, under the parking lot (spot 44).

The Parliament House—Stop in to see the grand hall with its fine hammer-beamed ceiling and stained glass (free). For a trip into the eighteenth century, drop by Tuesday through Friday around 10:00 or 10:30 a.m., the best time to see all the wigged and robed legal beagles hard at work. You are

welcome to observe trials in action (10:00 a.m.-4:00 p.m.).
The doorman is helpful (entry behind St. Giles Church near
parking spot 21, open daily to the public).

Museum of Childhood is a five-story playground of historical toys and games (free, 10:00 a.m.-6:00 p.m., till 5:00 p.m.
off-season, closed Sundays).

John Knox's House—Fascinating for Reformation buffs.
This fine sixteenth-century house is filled with things from
the life of the Great Reformer. (£1.25, Monday-Saturday
10:00 a.m.-4:30 p.m., firmly closed on Sunday.)

▲**Scottish Experience and Living Craft Centre**—This
commercial venture actually fills a void and, for many,
makes an entertaining visit. You'll see several crafts in
action (bagpipe making, weaving, pottery, kilt making), a
study-your-clan center, and an exhibit on Highland dress.
Finally, there's a cozy café/theater where you can have tea
and scones while watching one of four continuously running videos on Edinburgh or Scotland (£2, 10:00 a.m.-6:00
p.m., tel. 557-9350).

People's Story is an interesting exhibition tracing the lot of
the working class through the eighteenth, nineteenth, and
twentieth centuries (free, 10:00 a.m.-6:00 p.m., till 5:00 p.m.
off-season, closed Sundays).

▲**Huntly House**—Another old house full of old stuff,
worth a look for its early Edinburgh history. Don't miss the
copy of the National Covenant written on an animal skin or
the sketches of pre-Georgian Edinburgh with its lake still
wet (free, 10:00 a.m.-6:00 p.m., closed Sunday).

▲**Holyrood Palace**—At the bottom end of the Royal Mile,
this is where the queen stays when she's in town. On a
mandatory guided tour, see the royal apartments, state
apartment, lots of rich furnishings, paintings, and history
(£3, Monday-Saturday 9:30 a.m.-5:00 p.m., Sunday 10:30
a.m.-4:30 p.m. often closed when the queen's home, so ask
at the TI, tel. 556-7371).

Other Edinburgh Sightseeing Highlights
▲**Walter Scott Monument**—Built in 1840, this elaborate,
neo-Gothic monument honors the great author, one of

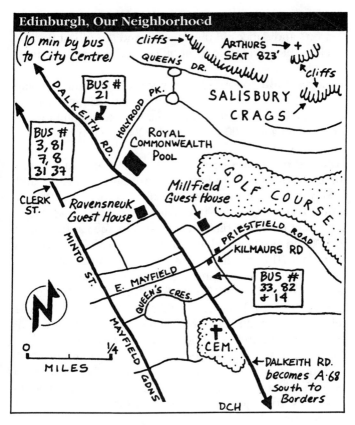

Edinburgh, Our Neighborhood

(10 min by bus to City Centre)

cliffs →

ARTHUR'S → SEAT 823'

QUEEN'S DR.

cliffs

SALISBURY CRAGS →

DALKEITH RD.

BUS # 21

HOLYROOD PK.

BUS # 3, 81 7, 8 31 37

ROYAL COMMONWEALTH POOL

GOLF COURSE

CLERK ST.

Ravensneuk Guest House

Millfield Guest House

MINTO ST.

PRIESTFIELD ROAD

KILMAURS RD

E. MAYFIELD

QUEEN'S CRES.

BUS # 33, 82 & 14

N

0   1/4

MILES

MAYFIELD GDNS.

CEM.

← DALKEITH RD. becomes A·68 South to Borders

DCH

Edinburgh's many illustrious sons. Climb 287 steps to a fine city orientation view (£1, 9:00 a.m.-6:00 p.m., until 5:00 p.m. off-season, closed Sunday).

▲▲**Georgian House** is a trip back to 1796. This refurbished Georgian house comes with a volunteer guide in each room who's bursting with stories and trivia. Start your visit with the interesting video (£2.80, 10:00 a.m.-5:00 p.m., Sunday 2:00-4:30 p.m., at 7 Charlotte Square). From this museum, walk through Georgian Edinburgh. The grand George Street, connecting St. Andrew and Charlotte Squares, was the centerpiece of the elegantly planned New Town.

Princes Street Gardens—This grassy former lake-bed separates Edinburgh's new and old towns with a wonderful escape from the city-ness of it all. There are plenty of concerts and dances in the summer and the oldest floral clock in the world. Join local office workers for a picnic lunch break.

National Gallery—An elegant neo-Classical building with a small, but impressive, collection of European master-pieces and the best look you'll get at Scottish paintings (free, 10:00 a.m.-5:00 p.m., Sunday 2:00-5:00 p.m., tel. 556-8921).

▲▲**Walking Tours**—Several competitive and hard-work-ing little companies do Royal Mile (usually 11:00 a.m. and 2:00 p.m.) and Ghost walks (usually 7:00 p.m. and 9:00 p.m.). Tours are about 90 minutes long and cost £3. Pick up brochures for Robin's (tel. 661-0125), Mercat (tel. 661-4541), and Heritage (tel. 659-5134). The Royal Mile is most important. The evening walks, more than a pile of ghost stories, are an entertaining and cheap night out.

▲**Hop On and Hop Off City Bus Tours**—Guide Friday (£5, tel. 556-2244) and LRT's "Edinburgh Classic Tour" (£4, tel. 220-4111) both circle the town center—Waverley Bridge, around the castle, Royal Mile, Calton Hill, Georgian town, and Princes Street—in about an hour with pick-ups about every 15 minutes and an informative narra-tion. You can stop and go all day on one ticket. On sunny days they go topless, but can suffer from traffic noise and congestion.

City Bus Tours—Several all-day bus tours can take you as far as Loch Ness. Tours leave from near the train sta-tion. "City, Sea, and Hills" is the best 2-hour tour of greater Edinburgh (£4, information at LRT office, on Waverley Bridge, tel. 220-4111).

Royal Commonwealth Games Swimming Pool—The biggest pool I've ever seen. Open to the public, good Café Aqua overlooking the pool, weights, saunas, plenty of water rides including Europe's biggest "flume" or water slide (£1.40, Monday-Friday 9:00 a.m.-9:00 p.m., Saturday and Sunday 8:00 a.m.-7:00 p.m., tel. 667-7211). If you'd rather go skiing, there's an open-all-year hill covered with brushes, with a chair lift, T-bar, and rentable skis, boots and poles, on the edge of town.

▲**Arthur's Seat**—A 30-minute hike up the 822-foot volcanic mountain (surrounded by a fine park overlooking Edinburgh), starting from the Holyrood Palace or the Commonwealth Pool, gives you a rewarding view. It's the easiest "I climbed a mountain" feeling I've ever had. You can drive up most of the way from behind; follow the one-way street from the palace.

Greyhound Races—This is a pretty low-brow scene. But if you've never seen dog racing, this is a memorable night out combining great dog- and people-watching with a chance to lose some money gambling. Races are held about two nights a week at Powderhall Stadium.

Edinburgh Crystal—Blowing, molding, cutting, polishing, engraving, the Edinburgh Crystal Company gives a great glassworks tour (it smashes Venice). Drive 10 miles south of town on A701 to Penicuik. The 35-minute tours start at regular intervals between 9:15 a.m. and 3:30 p.m., Monday-Friday (£3). There is a shop full of "bargain" second-quality pieces, a video show, and a good cafeteria. Consider catching the free coach shuttle service from Waverley Bridge (departures on the half-hour in summer) or doing it tomorrow on your way south. Call first. Tel. 0968/675128.

Stirling Castle—It's popular, but currently used as a barracks, and nowhere near as interesting as Edinburgh's castle. The town is pleasantly medieval, however, and many commute (1 hour by train) to the more hectic Edinburgh from here. (TI tel. 0786/475019.)

▲▲▲**The Edinburgh Festival**—One of Europe's great cultural events, Edinburgh's annual festival turns the city into a carnival of culture. There are enough music, dance, art, drama, and multicultural events to make even the most jaded tourist get frisky and drool with excitement. Every day is jammed with formal and spontaneous fun. The official and fringe festivals rage from mid-August through early September (August 14-September 3 in 1994), with the Military Tattoo starting a week earlier. Many city sights run on extended hours, and those that normally close on Sundays, don't. It's a glorious time to be in Edinburgh.

The official festival is more formal and serious with entertainment by festival invitation only. Although major events sell out well in advance, 10 to 15 percent of many event's seats are held to be sold at 8:00 a.m. on the day of the show at the show office at 21 Market Street (£4 to £35, CC-VMA, booking from April on, tel. 225-5756).

The more informal, "on the edge" comedy and theater, Fringe Festival (tel. 226-5259, bookings tel. 226-5138) has hundreds of events for which tickets are usually available at the door.

The Military Tattoo is a massing of the bands, drums, and bagpipes with groups from all over what was the British Empire. Displaying military finesse with a stirring lone-piper finale, this grand spectacle fills the castle esplanade nightly except Sunday throughout the festival (£8 to £15, CC-VMA, booking starts in January, tel. 225-1188). If nothing else, it is a really big show.

If you do manage to hit Edinburgh during the festival, add a third day and book a room far in advance. While fringe tickets and usually Tattoo tickets are available the day of the show, you may want to book an official event or two in advance. Do it direct by telephone, leaving your credit card number. You can pick up your ticket at the office the day of the show. Several publications list and evaluate festival events, including the festival's official schedule, the *Festival Times*, *The List*, *Fringe Program*, and the *Daily Diary*.

Shopping—The best shopping is along Princes Street (don't miss elegant old Jenner's Department Store), along Victoria Street (antiques galore), and the Royal Mile (touristy but competitively priced). Shops are usually open from 9:00 a.m. to 5:30 p.m. and later on Thursday.

▲▲**Folk Music**—Edinburgh offers folk music in pubs and more organized "Scottish folk evenings," generally in more expensive hotels. For £20 to £25 at several hotels on nearly any night you can enjoy a traditional—or at least what the tourists are led to believe is traditional—meal with the full slate of swirling kilts, blaring bagpipes, and colorful Scottish folk dancing. For an informal evening of folk music, find the right pub. My favorite Scottish band, the

North Sea Gas, plays (every Friday and many Saturdays, 8:30-11:00 p.m., free) at Platform One in the Caledonian Hotel on Princes Street.

Pubs that regularly feature folk music are the Fiddlers Arms (tel. 229-2665), White Hart Inn, and Black Bull (all on Grassmarket). Preservation Hall (a block away on Victoria Street, tel. 226-3816) is good for jazz and rock. Just off the Royal Mile on Cockburn Street, the Malt Shovel Pub is a typical Edinburgh pub with impromptu folk and jazz most nights and the best selection of malt whiskey in town (225-6843). The Edinburgh Folk Club, which meets at the cut-glass-elegant Café Royal (tel. 556-1884), is a good bet for traditional music and dancing.

Accommodations in Edinburgh (£1 = about $1.50, tel. code: 031)

The annual festival fills the city every year in the last half of August (August 14-September 3 in 1994). Conventions, school holidays, and other surprises can make room-finding tough at almost any time. After taking the grand tour of Edinburgh's budget accommodations it became clear to me that if you don't call in advance you'll probably end up paying 30 percent extra for a relative dump. The good places are a fine value. The rest are depressing. Call in advance! The TI room-finding service is an expensive last resort.

My favorite B&B district, where you'll find all these recommendations, is south of town near the Royal Commonwealth Pool, just off Dalkeith Road. It's a 20-minute walk from the Royal Mile, well-served by city buses (5 minutes and 50p to center; from Dalkeith Road, take red buses #12, 14, 21, 33, and 82 downtown), and all listings are on quiet streets a 2-minute walk from a bus stop.

These B&Bs are in a comfortably safe neighborhood with plenty of eateries, easy free parking, and a handy launderette (Monday-Friday 8:30 a.m.-5:00 p.m., Saturday and Sunday 10:00 a.m.-2:30 p.m., £2.30 for a self-serve load; for 50p more, they'll do it for you, and may even deliver, 208 Dalkeith Road, tel. 667-0825).

Most of these B&Bs have made a science out of perfect price discrimination and prices will vary with the seasonal demand. Going direct (rather than through the TI), you're likely to get the best price.

Millfield Guest House—Mrs. Liz Broomfield's place is thoughtfully furnished with antique class, a rare sit-and-chat ambience, and a comfy TV lounge. Since the showers are down the hall, you'll get spacious rooms (S-£15, D-£30, T-£45, a little more for one night only, good beds, absolutely no smoking, quiet but friendly, CC-VM, easy reservation with CC which lets you arrive late from Oban; 12 Marchhall Road, just east off Dalkeith Rd., EH16 5HR, tel. 031/667-4428). This is worth calling well in advance.

Ravensneuk Guest House is also good (D-£32 to £40 depending on room and season, family deals, solid beds, some non-smoking rooms; two doors off Dalkeith Road at 11 Blacket Ave., EH9 1RR, tel. 667-5347). Jeanette and Jim Learmonth rent seven rooms in this quiet, comfortable, and very Victorian home.

The Belford House is pretty basic and well-worn, but friendly and a better value than most places (D-£32, T-£48, family deals; 13 Blacket Avenue, next to Ravensneuk, tel. 667-2422, Mrs. Borthwick).

Dunedin Guest House is bright and pastel, nearly non-smoking, and a good value for those who need a private bathroom (S-£16 to £19, DB-£32 to £44 depending on the season, family deals, only five rooms, solid beds, TVs in rooms; 8 Priestfield Road, EH16 5HH, tel. 668-1949, Annette Preston).

Dorstan Private Hotel is small and personable, but professional and hotelesque with all the comforts. Several of its 14 rooms are on the ground floor. (DB-£50, DBWC-£60, family rooms, CC-VM; 7 Priestfield Road, EH16 5HJ, tel. 667-6721, fax 668-4644, Mairae Campbell).

The following places are sleepable in the same fine neighborhood, but a skimpier value, offering less person-ality for the same prices: **Highland Park House** (16 Kilmaurs Terrace, tel. 667-9204, Mrs. Cathy Kelly), **Kenvie Guest House** (D, DB, family rooms, 16 Kilmaurs Rd., EH16 5DA, tel. 668-1964), **"Amaragua" Guest House** (10

Kilmaurs Terrace, EH16 5DR, tel. 667-6775), and **Rosedene Guest House** (some *en suite* rooms, run by helpful Mr. Gallo, 4 Queen's Crescent, tel. 667-5806).

    Dorms and Hostels: Although Edinburgh's youth hostels are well run, open to all, and provide about a £7 savings over B&Bs, they include no breakfast and are comparatively scruffy and dreary. They are **The Bruntsfield Hostel** (on a park, 7 Bruntsfield Crescent, buses #11, #15, #16 to and from Princes St., tel. 447-2994), the **Edinburgh Hostel** (18 Eglinton Crescent, tel. 337-1120), the **High Street Independent Hostel** (£8.50 bunk beds with sheets in 8- to 10-bed rooms, young, hip, well-run, scruffy, videos, my mom wouldn't sleep a wink here, but my little sister would dig it, 50 yards off the Royal Mile, very central; 8 Blackfriars St., tel. 557-3984, free historic walks many mornings), and **Cowgate Tourist Hotel** (student dorms, open for tourists early July through mid-September, S-£10, £9 per bed in doubles and larger rooms, bleak, basic, but full of good services, kitchen, laundry; very central, just off Royal Mile, 112 The Cowgate, tel. 226-2153).

Food in Edinburgh by Neighborhood

Light Meals along the Royal Mile: Historic pubs and doily cafés with reasonable, rather unremarkable meals abound. **Deacon Brodie's Pub** serves good £5 meals upstairs (daily noon-9:00 p.m., crowded after 8:00 p.m.). For a cheap lunch in legal surroundings, try the cafeteria in the **Parliament House** (9:30 a.m.-3:00 p.m. Monday-Friday, entry behind St. Giles church near parking spot 21). Or munch prayerfully in the **Lower Aisle** restaurant under St. Giles church (10:00 a.m.-4:30 p.m.). **Clarinda's Tea Room**, near the bottom of the Royal Mile, is also good. On Victoria Street, consider the very French **Pierre Victoire** (at #9, tel. 225-1721) or the upstairs café in the Byzantium antique mall, across the street from Pierre Victoire. **Dubh Prais Restaurant** serves decent Scottish food in a small candlelit stone-walled basement (£15 and up, reserve in advance, chef/owner James McWilians, 123b High Street, tel. 557-5732).

Eating in the New Town: Edinburgh seems to be a lunching kind of place. Local office workers pile into **Lanterna** for good Italian food (family-run, fresh and friendly, 83 Hanover St., 2 blocks off Princes St., tel. 226-3090). Rose Street has tons of pubs. The **Waverley Center Food Court** (below the TI) is a ring of flashy, trendy, fast-food joints littered with paper plates and shoppers.

Dalkeith Road Area—Near Your B&B: For very good Scottish food, eat at **Unco Guid** (£14 meals, entertaining £23 five-course Scottish banquets with a 2-hour folk show two nights a week, across from Commonwealth Pool at 58 Dalkeith Rd., tel. 667-1816). For basic fish-and-chips, **Brattisanis** at 87 Newington Road (a block east of the pool) is good. Skip the milkshakes, but if you need some cheap haggis, they've got it. The **Chatterbox** (9:30 a.m. to 7:00 p.m., down Preston St. from the big pool) is fine for a light meal. The nearby **Wine Glass Pub** is the "in" place for the local crowd, with great atmosphere. The huge **Commonwealth Pool** has a noisy cafeteria for hungry swimmers and budget travelers (pass the entry without paying, sit with a poolside view).

EDINBURGH–HADRIAN'S WALL–DURHAM

Head south from Edinburgh, filling today with Britain's best Roman and Romanesque sights. After pondering Hadrian's Wall, ancient Rome's northernmost boundary, marvel at Durham's Cathedral, England's greatest Norman building, and enjoy an evensong service.

Suggested Schedule

9:00	Leave Edinburgh.
11:30	Arrive at Hadrian's Wall, tour the fort and Roman museum, walk along the wall, have lunch.
2:00	Drive to Durham.
4:00	Tour Durham cathedral.
5:15	Evensong service in cathedral.
6:30	Walk along riverside path near the cathedral.

Transportation: Edinburgh to Hadrian's Wall (100 miles) to Durham (50 miles)

From Edinburgh, Dalkeith Road leads south, becoming A68 (handy supermarket on left as you leave Dalkeith Town, 10 minutes south of Edinburgh, parking behind store). A68 takes you to Hadrian's Wall in 2 hours. You'll pass Jedburgh and its abbey after 1 hour. (For one last shot of shop-Scotland, there's a coach tour's delight just before Jedburgh, with kilt-makers, woolens, and a sheepskin shop.) Across from Jedburgh's lovely abbey is a free parking lot, a good visitor's center, and public toilets. The England/Scotland border (great view, Mr. Softy ice cream and tea caravan) is a fun quick stop. Before Hexham, roller-coaster 2 miles down A6079 to B6318, following the Roman wall westward. Notice the wall and its trenches on either side. After 10 minutes on B6318 and several "severe dips" (if there's a certified nerd or bozo in the car, these road signs add a lot to a photo portrait), pull into the Housesteads Roman Fort information center. The Roman fort is on the right.

After your visit, take the small road past Vindolanda (another Roman fort and museum) to A69. Go east past

Edinburgh–Hadrian's Wall–Durham

Hexham, then south on A68. The A690 takes you into Durham, conveniently hitting my recommended B&Bs. If you choose to squeeze the Beamish Museum (8 miles north of Durham) into today's plan, it's easy to find, located between the villages of Stanley and Chester-le-Street.

While there are a few parking spots right on the cathedral green, parking in old Durham is miserable. For a short stop, use the high-rise parking garage in the town center. From the garage's seventh floor, a walkway takes you right into the old town. Parking at my recommended B&Bs, a short walk from the center of Durham, is easy.

If you're using public transportation, head south on a train bound for Newcastle (2 hours, hourly). In summer, tour buses run between Newcastle and Hadrian's Wall (four daily). To visit the Wall by train, transfer at Newcastle, heading west to Bardon Mill (1 hour, hourly), the stop nearest Housesteads Fort. Return to Newcastle, then head south to Durham (15 minutes, hourly).

Sightseeing Highlights

▲▲▲Hadrian's Wall—One of England's most thought-provoking sights. During the reign of Emperor Hadrian, the Romans built this great stone wall around A.D. 130 to protect England from invading Scottish tribes. Stretching 74 miles from coast to coast, it was defended by nearly 20,000 troops.

Flanked by ditches, with castles every mile, the wall was built 15 feet high and wide enough to allow chariots to race from castle to castle. Today, several chunks of the wall, ruined forts, and museums thrill history buffs.

By far the best single stop is the Housesteads Fort with its fine museum, national park information center (£2, daily 10:00 a.m.-6:00 p.m., shorter hours off-season, with car park and snack bar, tel. 0434/344525), and the best-preserved segment of the wall, surrounded by powerful scenery. From Housesteads, hike west along the wall speaking Latin. Vindolanda, a larger Roman fort and museum, is just south of the wall and worth a visit only if you've devoured the Housesteads museum and are still hungry (tel. 0434/344277).

For a good 3-mile walk, go from Steel Rig (little road up from the Twice Brewed Pub) east along the crag and wall, past the mile castle sitting in a nick in the crag (castle #39, called Castle Nick), to Housesteads.

To sleep literally on the wall, the **Sewing Shields Farm B&B** is a great value (S-£14, D-£28, T-£42, family deals, evening meals; run by friendly Lyn Murray, just east of Housesteads Fort, Haydon Bridge, Hexham, NE47 6NW, tel. 0434/684418). The nearby Mile Castle Pub cooks up all sorts of exotic game and offers the best dinner around, according to hungry national park rangers. Two miles west of Housesteads, the **Twice Brewed Pub and Hotel** (S-£17, D-£34, plain dreary rooms, lots of singles, rarely full, tel. 0434/344534) serves decent pub grub to a local crowd. The comfortable **Once Brewed Youth Hostel** (£8 per bed, with breakfast, tel. 0434/344360) is just next to the Twice Brewed Pub.

▲▲Beamish Open-Air Museum—see Day 20.

▲▲**Durham Cathedral**—Built to house the much-venerated bones of St. Cuthbert from Lindisfarne, the church is the best, least altered Norman cathedral in England (free, 7:15 a.m.-7:30 p.m. daily, limited access during services). Study the difference between this heavy Romanesque ("Norman" is British for Romanesque) fortress of worship and the light-filled Gothic of later centuries (like York's Minster, tomorrow). Let one of the many church attendants show you around. Pick up the 30p guide, find the tombs of St. Cuthbert and Bede, and see the audiovisual introduction (50p, 11:00 a.m.-3:00 p.m.). The treasury is filled with medieval bits and holy pieces (£1, 10:00 a.m.-4:30 p.m., Sunday 2:00-4:30 p.m.). The view from the tower is worth the 300 steps (£1, 10:00 a.m.-4:00 p.m., closed Sunday). There's also a good cafeteria.

For a thousand years this cradle of English Christianity has been praising God. To experience the cathedral in its intended context, go for an evensong service. Arrive early and ask to be seated in the choir. You're in the middle of a spiritual Oz as forty boys sing psalms—a red-and-white-robed pillow of praise, raised up by the powerful pipe organ. You've got elephant-sized ears as the beautifully-carved choir stalls function as giant sound scoops facing grunting and trumpeting pipes, each with an agenda. If you're lucky and the service went well, the organist runs a spiritual victory lap as the congregation breaks up. (No offering plates, no sermon, 5:15 almost nightly, 3:30 p.m. Sunday, tel. 091/386-2367.)

The old town of Durham, bordered on three sides by its river, cuddles the cathedral. It has a workaday medieval cobbled atmosphere and a scraggly peasant's market just off the main square, but is exciting mostly for its cathedral. Shoppers not charmed by the Middle Ages are thrilled by England's biggest mall, the Metro Centre, in nearby Newcastle.

For a 20-minute woodsy escape, walk Durham's riverside path from Framwelgate Bridge to Prebends Bridge. Just between the Prebends Bridge and the old town, you'll find "The Upper Room," a cluster of trees carved to show the Last Supper when seen from the tree-trunk throne provided.

Holy Island and Bamburgh—For this detour, leave Edinburgh by going around Arthur's Seat Park. At Holyrood Palace, you'll pick up the A1. Follow the signs along the coast. After 50 miles of A1, take the small road to the Holy Island of Lindisfarne Gospels fame. Twelve hundred years ago, this was Christianity's toehold on England. It's a pleasant visit, a quiet town with an evocative priory and striking castle, reached by a 2-mile causeway that is cut off daily by high tides. The striking castle is not worth touring. Tidal charts are posted, warning you when this holy place becomes Holy Island and you become stranded (for tide information, tel. 0289/307283). For a peaceful overnight, consider Holy Island. A few good B&Bs cluster in the town center (**Britannia Guest House**, D-£26, DB-£30, only three rooms, tel. 0289/89218). A few miles farther south down the coast is the grand Bamburgh Castle overseeing the most lovely stretch of beach in Britain. Its impressive interior is worth touring (£2.40, daily noon-5:00 p.m., April-October, tel. 06684/208). Berwick TI, tel. 0289/330733.

Accommodations in Durham (£1 = about $1.50, tel code: 091)

Durham is small. The train station is a 10-minute walk uphill from the center where everything is clustered safely within the protective and tight bend in the river (TI on the town square, Monday-Friday 9:00 a.m.-6:30 p.m., Saturday 9:00 a.m.-5:00 p.m., Sunday 2:00-5:00 p.m., often posts B&B vacancies on its door after hours, tel. 091/384-3720). My recommended B&Bs are along Crossgate (from the city center, cross Framwelgate Bridge, take the first left, up the hill), a 5-minute walk from the market square and the train station. "Pay peanuts, get monkeys" places are along Claypath (over the highway from the TI).

Colebrick B&B, meticulously run by Freda Mellanby, is a modern comfortable home with two double rooms for rent. Everything is super comfortable and on the ground level (D-£40, solid beds, non-smoking, garden with cathedral views; 21 Crossgate, Durham DH1 4PS, tel. 384-9585). Husband Robin, son Stuart, and faithful dog Emma also help out.

Castleview Guest House is a block closer to the center, bigger and creakier with seven comfortable rooms and a classy lounge (S-£20, D-£35, DB-£45, T-£40; 4 Crossgate, DH1 4PS, tel. 386-8852, Mike and Anne Williams).

Castledene B&B is tidy, simple, and friendly with three rooms and a TV lounge (S-£16, twin-£32; continue up Crossgate to Palatine View, cross the street, go up 10 steps to the pedestrian lane and walk 100 yards parallel and above Crossgate Peth to the last house, 37 Nevilledale Terrace, tel. 384-8386, Lorna Byrne). Mrs. McGee rents decent rooms on a busier street closer to the station (S-£15, D-£30, T-£45; 53 Hawthorn Terrace, DH1 4EQ, tel. 384-7601).

The **Durham Castle** is a student residence actually on the castle grounds facing the cathedral. It rents 100 singles and 30 doubles to travelers from July through September (£17 per person, £21 with private facilities, meals served in an elegant dining hall; parking, with luck, on the cathedral green; tel. 374-3863). Request a room in the classy old main building. Otherwise you may get bomb-shelter-style modern dorm rooms.

For dinner, trust your host's advice. There are several interesting places in the town center. **Shaheens** in the old post office, up Saddler Street, serves good Indian meals with a healthy twist, nightly from 6:00. **The Stones**, on Silver Street, is a trendy 1960s burger place. **The Dragon**, out Claypath, serves good pub grub. **The Duke of Wellington** (1½ miles down the A1050/Darlington Road) serving great (and big-enough-for-two) meals in great pub atmosphere, is worth the drive.

BEAMISH OPEN-AIR MUSEUM OR NORTH YORK MOORS TO YORK

Spend this morning either reliving the North Yorkshire turn-of-the-century or getting a good dose of the stark beauty of the North York Moors and James Herriot country. Then set up and orient yourself in York, one of England's most exciting cities.

Suggested Schedule

9:30	Leave your Durham B&B.
10:00	Tour the Beamish Open-Air Museum (or get an earlier start and head into the Moors).
3:00	Set up in York (2-hour drive from Beamish).
4:00	Tour Railway Museum (open until 6:00 p.m.).
6:30	Dinner on Gillygate and walk the wall. Or grab a quick bite and catch the free 7:00 p.m.city walking tour (from TI).

Transportation: Durham to York (80 miles)

Beamish is 8 miles north of Durham. It's well sign-posted, located between Chester-le-Street and Stanley. For York, drive A167, A1, and A59 to York's Ring Road. Circle north (left), then follow A19 into town. It becomes Bootham and you'll find your B&B just before Bootham hits York's medieval town gate. Consider turning your rental car in upon arrival in York. You won't use it tomorrow, and train connections are great from York to Cambridge (2½ hours, leaves almost hourly, with a change in Petersborough) and York to London (2 hours, hourly, £44).

Shuttle buses connect downtown Durham and the Beamish Museum regularly. Trains zip from Durham to York hourly, getting you there in an hour.

Sightseeing Highlights

▲▲Beamish Open-Air Museum—This huge, unique center energetically takes its visitors back to turn-of-the-century Northumbria. You'll need at least 3 hours to explore the 1900 town, train station, school, mining camp,

and working farm. This isn't wax; if you touch the
exhibits, they may slap you. Attendants at each stop
explain everything, and an old tramway shuttles you
through the huge park, saving wear and tear on your feet
(£7; daily 10:00 a.m.-6:00 p.m., mid-July through August,
last tickets sold at 4:00; shoulder season until 5:00, last
entry at 3:00; winter until 4:00 and closed Monday and
Friday; hourly buses from Durham; tel. 0207/231811).
Unique in its coverage of the dawn of our century,
Beamish is a former "European museum of the year."

▲**North York Moors: Danby Lodge**—If you decide to
explore the moors, the North York Moors Visitors Centre
provides the best orientation. It's a grand old lodge offering exhibits, shows, and nature walks, an information
desk with plenty of books and maps, brass-rubbing, a
cheery cafeteria, and brochures on several good walks
that start right there (free, daily 10:00 a.m.-5:00 p.m.,
April-October, tel. 0287/660654).

North Yorkshire Moors Railway—If you're tired of
driving (or without wheels), this 18-mile, 50-minute
steam engine ride from Grosmont and Goathland to Pick-
ering goes through some of the best parts of the moors
almost hourly. Unfortunately, the windows are small and
dirty (wipe off the outside of yours before you roll), and
the tracks are in a scenic gully (£9, tel. 0751/72508). Picker-
ing, with its rural-life museum, castle, and Monday market,
is worth a stop.

▲**Hutton-le-Hole**—This postcard-pretty town is home of
the fine little Ryedale Museum, which illustrates "farm life
in the moors" through reconstructed and furnished eighteenth-century local buildings (daily 10:30 a.m.-5:30 p.m.,
April-October, tel. 07515/367). Car park and public toilets
are nearby.

Castle Howard—Especially popular since the filming of
Brideshead Revisited, this is a fine palatial home but about
half as interesting as Blenheim (late March-October).

Rievaulx Abbey—A highlight of the North York Moors,
but a rerun of fine old abbeys you've already seen.

▲**James Herriot country** is in Yorkshire Dales National
Park, just west of the North York Moors. Tourist offices

have a brochure called "The Herriot Trail, a Circular Drive from Richmond through the valleys of Wensleydale, Swaledale and Arkengarthdale." To reach the Herriot Trail, leave Durham heading south on A1, take A6108 to Richmond, and turn onto B6270. The village of Reeth (where much of the Herriot series was filmed) is worth a stop. Reeth's Black Bull pub serves good and interesting food. Between Reeth and Feetham turn left, following the lane over the top of the moors to the village of Askrigg. Then, after Bainbridge, turn left on A684, heading east to Leyburn, where you'll take the A6108 through Middleham, Masham, and Abednego, passing the ruined abbey of Jervaulx, to Ripon and on into York.

▲**Or a stop on the East Coast**—A short drive from the moors, **Whitby** is a fun resort town with a busy harbor, steep and salty old streets, and a carousel of Coney Island-type amusements. It has lots of B&Bs, a great abbey (next door to a good youth hostel: £6.50, 70 beds, about 10 beds per room, tel. 0947/602878), and a colorful people scene. **Pannett House** is a good value, renting nine rooms, a 10- or 15-minute walk from the harbor action (S-£12, D-£24, T-£36; 14 Normanby Terrace, tel. 0947/603261, Val and Allan Perks). TI tel. 0947/602674.

▲**Staithes**—Captain James Cook's boyhood town, this is a salty tumble of cottages bunny-hopping down a ravine into a tiny harbor. Fishermen still outnumber tourists in undiscovered Staithes. The only reason I'd go to Staithes is to spend the night. The charming 200-year old **Cobble Cottage** rents four twin rooms on the waterfront (D-£32, cheaper for two nights; 3 Church Street, tel. 0947/840297, Maureen and Ken Hart). The **Harborside Guest House**, also on the waterfront, provides basic beds and the sound of waves to lull you to sleep (D-£38, four rooms, tel. 0947/841296). There's good bar food at the Royal George on High Street. The Endeavour Restaurant, also right downtown, is even better. Staithes is four villages north of Whitby, a short ride from the moors.

York—see Day 21.

YORK

On this very busy York day, start with a good look at York's great cathedral, wander through its wonderfully preserved medieval quarter, and spend the last half of the day immersed in the past—first reliving the 1800s in the Castle Museum, then going all the way back to the year 994, to visit the town the Vikings called Jorvik.

Suggested Schedule

9:00	Tour York Minster.
10:00	Browse through the old town and the Shambles (or catch the walking tour if you didn't last night).
2:00	York Castle Museum.
6:00	Jorvik Viking Center.

Orientation

York is big only in historical terms. Everything—the sights, train station, TI, and B&Bs—is within a few minutes' walk. Don't even think of taking the car through the old city gates. All recommended B&Bs have parking. There's a long-term car park near Bootham, the road that you'll follow into town. The center of York is virtually traffic-free and a busker-filled joy for walking. The farthest walk a visitor would make (from B&B, across the old town to the Castle Museum) takes no more than 15 minutes.

In York, a "bar" is a gate and a "gate" is a street (from the Norse, a reminder of the town's Viking heritage). Bootham Bar (a gate in the medieval town wall) is the hub of your York visit. At Bootham Bar (or on Exhibition Square facing it), you'll find the TI, most walking-tour and tour-bus starting points, and handy access to the medieval town wall, Gillygate (lined with good eateries). The Minster (cathedral), all my recommended B&Bs, the train station, and Railway Museum are all within 5 blocks.

At the tourist office, pick up the 50p mini-guide and map and the free *What's On*. Ask about special events and confirm your sightseeing plans (Monday-Saturday 9:00

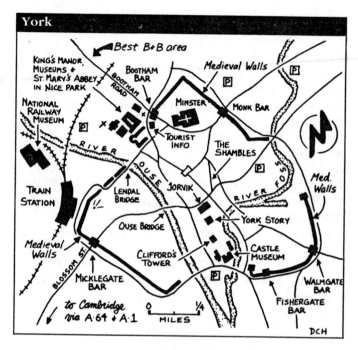

York

Best B+B area

King's Manor, Museums + St. Mary's Abbey in Nice Park

National Railway Museum

Bootham Bar

Bootham Road

Medieval Walls

Minster

Monk Bar

Tourist Info

The Shambles

River Ouse

Jorvik

River Foss

Med. Walls

Train Station

Lendal Bridge

Ouse Bridge

York Story

Medieval Walls

Blossom St.

Clifford's Tower

Castle Museum

Walmgate Bar

Micklegate Bar

to Cambridge via A·64 + A·1

Fishergate Bar

0   ¼
MILES

DCH

a.m.-7:00 p.m., Sunday 10:00 a.m.-1:00 p.m. in summer, Monday-Saturday 9:00 a.m.-5:00 p.m., closed Sunday the rest of the year, tel. 0904/621756). There is a smaller TI at the train station. The TI offers a £1 family "discount to the sights" card.

Sightseeing Highlights

▲▲▲**Walking Tours**—Charming local volunteer guides give energetic and entertaining free two-hour walks through York (daily at 10:15 a.m. and 2:15 p.m. April-October, plus 7:00 p.m. June-August, leaving from the TI). These are better than the gimmicky commercial walks. There are many other York walking tours. The ghost tours, offered after nightfall, are popular (but the evening free walks throw in a few ghosts also). The TI has produced three entertaining tape-recorded "Yorspeed" tours. You rent a tape and a Walkman and have a day to follow your recorded guide through "The Streets," around "The Walls," or with "The Ghosts," (about 2 hours per tape, £4 for one, £4.50 for two, tel. 652653, from the train station TI or the Bootham Bar TI).

▲**Guide Friday Hop-on and Hop-off bus tours**—As in Bath, Edinburgh and Stratford, York's Guide Friday offers tour guides on speed who can talk enthusiastically to three sleeping tourists in a gale on a topless double-decker bus for an hour without stopping. Buses make the hour-long circuit, covering much that the city walking tours don't (£5 for all day, departures every 10 or 15 minutes from 9:20 a.m. until around 6:00 p.m., tel. 640896). While you can hop on and off where you like, unlike the other towns, the York route is of no value from a transportation-to-the-sights point of view. I'd catch it at the TI and ride it all the way around or get off at the Railway Museum, skipping the last 5 minutes.

▲**City Walls**—The historic walls of York provide a fine 2-mile walk. Be sure to walk from Bootham Bar (gate) to Monk Bar for outstanding cathedral views. Open until dusk and free.

▲▲**The National Railway Museum**—This thunderous museum shows 150 fascinating years of British railroad history. Fanning out from a grand roundhouse are an array of historic cars and engines, including Queen Victoria's lavish royal car and the very first "stagecoaches on rails." There's much more, including exhibits on dining cars, post cars, Pullman cars, train posters, and videos. This is the biggest and best railroad museum anywhere (£4, Monday-Saturday 10:00 a.m.-6:00 p.m., Sunday 11:00 a.m.-6:00 p.m., tel. 621261).

▲▲▲**The York Minster (cathedral)**—The pride of York, this largest Gothic church in Britain is a brilliant example of how the High Middle Ages were far from dark. Pick up the "Welcome to the York Minster" flyer at the information desk. Take advantage of the helpful blue-armbanded Minster Guides. Free hour-long guided tours leave about hourly (fewer on Saturday, none on Sunday). The east window is the largest medieval glass window in existence. For most, the chapter room and the crypt are not worth the admission. But the tower (£2, long climb, great view) and the undercroft/treasury (£1.80) are. The undercroft gives you a chance to climb down, archaeologically and physically, through the centuries to see the roots of the much smaller but still huge Norman (Romanesque, 1100) church which stood on this spot, and below that, to the Roman excavations. Constantine was proclaimed Roman emperor here in A.D. 306. The undercroft also give you a look at the modern concrete save-the-church foundations. The cathedral is open daily, 7:30 a.m. to 8:30 p.m.. The chapter room, tower, and undercroft have shorter hours, usually 10:00 a.m.-3:30 p.m.. Evensong is daily at 5:00 p.m. (4:00 on Saturday and Sunday), but often without the "song" (usually spoken on Wednesday and Saturday). While a donation of £1.50 is reasonably requested, if I'm visiting the undercroft or climbing the tower, I give it (and more) in the form of those admissions. Tel. 624426.

▲**The Shambles**—This is the most colorful old York street in the half-timbered core of town. Ye olde downtown York is very touristy, but a window-shopping, people-watcher's delight.

▲▲▲**York Castle Museum**—Truly one of Europe's top museums, this is a walk with Dickens, the closest thing to a time-tunnel experience England has to offer. It includes a magnificent collection of old shops well-stocked exactly as they were 150 years ago, costumes, armor, an incredible Anglo-Saxon helmet (from A.D. 750), and the "every home needs one" exhibit showing the evolution of vacuum cleaners, toilets, TVs, bicycles, stoves, and so on, from their crude beginnings to now. (£4, 9:30 a.m.-5:30 p.m., Sunday 10:00 a.m.-5:30 p.m., cafeteria, shop, car park; the £2 guidebook is unnecessary, but a nice souvenir, tel. 653611).

▲▲**Jorvik**—The innovative museum of Viking York takes you back a thousand years—literally backward—in a little Disney-type train car. Then, still seated, you cruise slowly for 13 minutes through the sounds, sights, and even smells of the re-created Viking village of Jorvik. Next your little train takes you through the actual excavation sight (best Viking dig I've seen anywhere), then lets you off to browse through a gallery of Viking shoes, combs, locks, and other intimate glimpses of that red-headed culture (£4, daily 9:00 a.m.-7:00 p.m., November-March 9:00 a.m.-5:00 p.m., tel. 643211. Don't be pressured into buying the colorful guidebook with your ticket. To minimize time in line—which can be more than an hour—go very early (at 8:45 a.m.) or very late. In summer the last entrance is 7:00 p.m. Day-trippers make summer midday lines routinely 2 hours long. Jorvik is not worth even a 30-minute wait. Get there at 6:00 p.m. and you'll sail right in. Some love this "ride"; others call it a gimmicky rip-off. While it has inspired a chain of copy-cat historical rides around England, most of which are also gimmicky rip-offs, I like Jorvik.

Honorable mention: York has a number of other sights and activities (described in the TI's "Mini-guide and Map") which pale in comparison to the big four, but are worth a look if you have the time. The York Story (£1.40, associated with, across the street from, and pushed by the Castle Museum) is an exhibit displaying the city's past, with a 45-minute video on the history of York. It's good, straight history.

Accommodations in York (£1 = about $1.50, tel. code: 0904)

I've listed peak season prices. Outside of the peak July-August months, York B&B prices get soft and some places may drop by several pounds. I've limited my recommen-dations to the handiest B&B neighborhood, just outside the old town wall's Bootham gate, along the road called Bootham. All are within about 5 minutes' walk of the Minster, train station, and TI. They are small, family-run, will generally hold a room with a phone call, work hard to help their guests sightsee and eat smartly, have lots of fairly steep stairs, and are on quiet, residential side streets. Parking is generally no problem. Most places have their own spots or loaner permits for street parking. The train tracks bordering many places are used by the little Scarborough train which doesn't run at night. There's a handy coin-op Clifton Launderette on Bootham.

York, Our Neighborhood

CLIFTON LAUNDROMAT
CLAREMONT
TO B·1363 HELMSLEY & MOORS
QUEEN ANNE'S TERRACE
N
QUEEN ANNE SCHOOL
YARDS
PORTLAND
BOOTHAM TERRACE
ST. MARY'S
SCHOOL
SYCAMORE
BOOTHAM
GILLYGATE
MEDIEVAL WALL
BOOTHAM BAR
YORK MINSTER
SYCAMORE TERR.
LONG FIELD
MARYGATE
ART GALLERY
EX. SQ.
HIGH PETERGATE
TOURIST INFO.
PARKING
FREDERIC
KING'S MANOR
ST. MARY'S ABBEY RUINS
MUSEUM GARDENS
ST. LEONARD'S
MUSEUM ST.
RIVER HOUSE
WALK TO STATION
TO RAILROAD MUSEUM
LEEMAN
TO STATION

① AIRDEN HOUSE
② THE SYCAMORE
③ ASTORIA HOUSE
④ CLAREMONT GUEST HOUSE
⑤ THE HAZELWOOD
⑥ WHITE DOVES
⑦ 23 SAINT MARY'S
⑧ QUEEN ANNE'S GUEST HOUSE
⑨ ST. MARY'S HOTEL
⑩ COACH HOUSE PUB
⑪ ELLIOT'S HOTEL PUB
⑫ BOWLING GREEN

Airden House—Susan and Keith keep this snug and traditional place simple and friendly. They are a great source
of local travel tips. Airden House, the most central of these
Bootham-area listings, has eight rooms, a grandfather clock-
cozy TV lounge, and brightness and warmth throughout.
Their two *en suite* doubles are way up on top. (D-£34, DB-
£40; 1 St. Mary's, York Y03 7DD, tel. 638915).

The Sycamore, run by Margaret and David Tyce, is a
fine value with small cozy rooms and plenty of personal
touches, right across from a fun-to-watch bowling green
(D-£30, DB-£35, family deals, no lounge; 19 Sycamore
Place off Bootham Terrace, YO3 7DW, tel. 624712).

Astoria Hotel—Mr. and Mrs. Bradley offer 17 rooms in
an old, well-worn, but decent place (S-£16, SB-£16, D-£30,
DB-£35, family deals, CC-V; 6 Grosvenor Terrace, Bootham,
York, Y03 7AG, tel. 0904/659 558).

Claremont Guest House is a friendly, non-smoking house offering three rooms, thoughtful touches, and solid beds (D-£30, DB-£40; 18 Claremont Terrace off Gillygate, YO3 7EJ, tel. 625158, Gill and Martyn Cornell).

The Hazelwood is my most hotelesque listing. Joy and Peter Cox run this elegant and spacious old 16-room place in a stately, very proper way, paying careful attention to details and serving a classy breakfast. (S-£21, D-£37, DWC-£37, DBWC-£45, DBWC with four-poster-£50, family deals, CC-VM, non-smoking, one ground floor room, reserve by letter; 24 Portland St, Gillygate, YO3 7EH, tel. 626548, fax 628032).

White Doves is a cheery little place, with four bright and comfy rooms (DB-£36, 20 Claremont Terrace off Gillygate, YO3 7EJ, tel. 625957, Pauline Pearce).

23 St. Marys is a rococo riot. Mrs. Hudson has done everything super-correctly, and offers nine rooms with strong beds, modern facilities, and all the doily touches (SB-£28, DB-£48, no smoking; 23 St. Mary's, YO3 7DD, tel. 622738).

Queen Anne's Guest House is compact, clean, and cheery (D-£28, DB-£30; 24 Queen Anne's Road, tel. 629-389). For similar prices, you could try **Arron Guest House** (42 Bootham Crescent, tel. 625-927). **St. Mary's Hotel** is a decent non-smoking place (D-£30, DB-£40, CC-V; 17 Longfield Terrace, tel. 626972).

The Golden Fleece—For a funky, murky, creaky experience right in the center of the old town, consider this historic 400-year-old pub that rents five rooms upstairs (pub closed at 11:00 p.m.). The floors aren't level, the beds are four-posters, and the local crowd fills the ground-floor pub with smoke and belly laughs (D-£37, family room with a four-poster and bunks, one-person jacuzzi in the shared bathroom, private car park; 16 Pavement, York, YO1 2ND, tel. 625171).

York's **Youth Hotel** (D-£24, £8 in 4- to 6-bed dorms, 11 Bishophill Senior Road, York YO1 1EF, tel. 625904 or 630613) is clean, cheery, well-run, with lots of extras like a kitchen, laundromat, games, and bar. They take no telephone reservations, but normally have beds until noon.

Eating in York
Near Bootham Bar and your B&B: For pub dinners, consider the **Coach House** (6:30-9:30 nightly, 20 Marygate, tel. 652780), **Elliot's Hotel Restaurant and Pub** (just off Bootham Terrace), or one of several pubs on Gillygate. Gillygate, which starts at Bootham Bar, is lined with interesting, cheap, healthy and/or fun eateries: **Mamma Mia's** (#20 Gillygate, daily 11:30 a.m.-2:00 p.m. and 5:30-11:00 p.m.) is great for Italian. A popular extremely vegetarian place is across the street and the **Phoenix** cooks first-class Chinese (eat-in or take-out). There's also a traditional little "chippie" (fish-and-chips joint) where tattooed people eat in and house-bound mothers take out. Or go with the latest pub grub advice from the people who run your B&B.

For a reasonable, historic, handy lunch, try the **King's Manor** on Exhibition Square (through the courtyard on the left, lunch only, noon-2:00 p.m., Monday-Friday). The tea room at the **Bootham Bar Hotel** (10:00 a.m.-5:30 p.m. daily, 4 High Petergate, near the TI) serves a tasty and reasonable lunch.

For good meals downtown: Consider one of several places along the street called Pavement. The **Golden Fleece** pub is a hopping place serving famous Yorkshire Pudding and hearty meals until 10:00 p.m.. Next door, the **York Pie Shop** does traditional meat pies well. **Kites**, closer to the center, on Grape Lane, serves tasty, fresh, and unusual French and English meals at good prices. **Ye Olde Starre Inn**, the oldest pub in town, has yet to learn the art of cooking.

York is famous for its elegant teahouses. Around four-ish, drop into one for tea and cakes. **Betty's** is most famous, with people lining up to get in, but several others can satisfy your king- or queen-for-a-day desires.

YORK–CAMBRIDGE–LONDON

On this final day, you travel 200 miles from York to London with a stop in Cambridge, renowned for its famous universities and A+ architecture. Completing your circle of Britain, spend your last night in London, where you started three weeks ago.

Suggested Schedule	
8:00	Leave York for Cambridge.
12:00	Take the walking tour.
2:00	Lunch and visit King's College Chapel.
4:00	Free to explore, stroll through the Backs, shop in the center, go punting, or take a quick look at the Fitzwilliam Museum paintings.
7:00	Catch the 60-minute train ride to London (confirm times at the station). Tube or taxi to your London hotel. Tour over. Everybody off the bus!

Transportation: York to Cambridge (150 miles) to London (50 miles)

Cambridge is a 4-hour drive from York. From York, head north on Bootham to the Ring Road, circle left, exit on A64, direction Leeds, and in 10 miles get on the A1 to Cambridge. There's a tempting motorway (M1) farther west, but stick to the A1, which is near-motorway quality and a more interesting drive. Cambridge's huge, central Short Stay Parking Lot is handy. From Cambridge, if you're driving to London, any major road going west or south will direct you to the M11 motorway. It's 60 high-speed miles (with no gas stations) to the London ring road. Catch the poorly-marked M25 outer ring road (you'll see Heathrow and Gatwick signs) and circle around to the best position to start your central attack. (You can buy a good London map at the Cambridge TI for 95p.)

If you do decide to drive into London—where your car is a useless headache—you'll learn why I recommend leaving your car in York or Cambridge. You can take the train from York to Cambridge (2½ hours, almost hourly, with a change in Petersborough) or do Cambridge as a side trip from London's Liverpool Station (60 minutes, two trains hourly, £12 one-way or round-trip).

To reach the center of town from the Cambridge train station, take a £2.50 taxi ride, 20-minute walk, or easy and fast-as-a-taxi "City Rail Link" shuttle bus (60p, every 8 minutes, direct to Emmanuel Street).

To get from York to London's airports, take the train into London and connect from there (good connections, see below). There are direct bus connections from Cambridge to Heathrow and Gatwick airports.

Cambridge

Sixty miles north of London, this historic town of 100,000 people is world-famous for its prestigious university. Wordsworth, Isaac Newton, Tennyson, Darwin, and Prince Charles are a few products of this busy brain-works. More pleasant than its rival, Oxford, Cambridge is the epitome of a university town, with busy bikers, stately halls of residence, plenty of bookshops, and proud locals who can point out where electrons and DNA were discovered and where the first atom was split.

Cambridge is small but congested. There are two main streets separated from the river by the most interesting colleges. The town center has a TI, colorful marketplace, and several parking lots. Everything is within a pleasant walk. Use the TI (Monday-Friday 9:00 a.m.-6:00 or 7:00 p.m.; Saturday 9:00 a.m.-5:00 p.m.; summer Sundays 10:30 a.m.-3:30 p.m., Wheeler St., tel. 0223/322640). Remember, the university dominates—and owns—most of Cambridge. Approximate term schedule is January 15 through March 15, April 15 through June 8, and October 8 through December 8. The colleges are closed to visitors during exams, from mid-April until late June. But the town is never sleepy.

Sightseeing Highlights

▲▲**Walking Tour of the Colleges**—The best way to understand Cambridge's town-gown rivalry and to be sure of getting a good run-down on the historic and scenic high-lights of the university—as well as some fun local gossip—is to take the walking tour. It's run by and leaves from the tourist office (July and August tours at 11:00, noon, 1:00, 2:00, and 3:00; the rest of the year, only at 11:00 and 2:00). The 11:00 a.m. and 1:00 p.m. tours spend a third of their time in King's College Chapel, which you could do on your own. Other tours have more time for more variety. Tours cost £3.30 (or £5 for the ones that do KCC). Telephone to reserve a tour a day in advance (and ask about the route to know if you should visit KCC and/or Trinity's Wren Library on your own). You'll need to pick up the ticket 30 minutes early. Private guides are also available. Guide Friday hop-on and hop-off bus tours (£6, departing every 15 minutes) are informative and cover the outskirts whereas walking tours go where buses can't, right in the center.

▲▲**King's College Chapel**—View the single most impressive building in town, high Gothic at its best, with the most medieval stained glass in any one spot, 2,000 tons of incredible fan vaulting and Rubens's great Adoration of the Magi. (£2, erratic hours depending on school and events, but generally 9:30 a.m.-4:30 p.m.) During term you're welcome to enjoy the 5:30 p.m. evensong service (Tuesday-Saturday) at King's College Chapel.

▲▲**Trinity College**—Half of Cambridge's 63 Nobel Prize winners came from this richest and biggest of the town's colleges. Don't miss the Wren-designed library with its wonderful carving and fascinating original manuscripts (free, open Monday-Friday noon-2:00 p.m., Saturday 10:30 a.m.-12:30 p.m.). Just outside the library entrance, Sir Isaac Newton, who spent 30 years at Trinity, clapped his hands and timed the echo to measure the speed of sound as it raced down the side of the cloister and back. In the library you can read Newton's hand-written account of this, alongside the original hand-written Winnie-the-Pooh.

▲▲**Fitzwilliam Museum**—The best museum of antiquities and art outside of London, the Fitzwilliam has fine Impressionist paintings, old manuscripts, and Greek, Egyptian, and Mesopotamian collections (free; antiquities open Tuesday-Saturday 10:00 a.m.-2:00 p.m. and paintings 2:00-5:00 p.m.; everything on Sunday 2:15-5:00 p.m.; closed Monday; tel. 332900).

Museum of Classical Archeology—While this has no originals, it offers a unique chance to see accurate copies (from nineteenth-century casts of the originals) of virtually every famous ancient Greek and Roman statue (over 600 statues, free, 9:00 a.m.-5:00 p.m. Monday-Friday, Sidgwick Ave., tel. 335153).

▲**Punting on the Cam**—For a little levity and probably more exercise than you really want, try hiring one of the traditional flat-bottom punts from stalls near either bridge and pole yourself up and down (around and around, more likely) the lazy Cam. Once you get the hang of it, it's a fine way to enjoy the scenic side of Cambridge. After 5:00 p.m., it's less crowded/embarrassing.

Posttour London

Remember to call your airline to reconfirm your return flight three days in advance, leaving your London hotel's phone number for any messages.

If you've planned ahead, taking advantage of the opportunity to reserve hard-to-get tickets at the start of your trip, you'll enjoy a special show or event before returning home.

Ask at your hotel for the easiest way to get to the airport. To Gatwick, take the shuttle train from Victoria Station. To Heathrow, take the tube or the Airbus. The Airbus is easier, dropping you right at the appropriate terminal (£5). For rides to the airports, taxis are usually a rip-off, but two or three people in a hurry can ride for a reasonable fare from the West End out. Locals can usually negotiate a £15 ride to Heathrow from an un-metered cab or a hungry black one.

Call before going out to the airport to check for delays. Call home (50p is enough) to say all's well and what time you're due in. You'll arrive home at almost the same time you left London, considering the hours you gain in westward flight.

As you roar down the runway and wing homeward, you'll savor the memories of the best 22 days Britain has to offer—and know you've only scratched the surface.

The obvious gap in this 22-day plan is Ireland. I love Ireland, but it doesn't make Britain's top 22 days. Still, Ireland is easy to work in as a side-trip or finale to this 22-day plan. A visit of two or three days isn't really worth the time and expense to get there. I'd plan on a week or nothing at all.

Itinerary Strategy—Getting There

Ireland can easily be inserted into the 22-day plan from Scotland, North Wales, or London. Scotland's Glasgow has great bus-ferry-bus connections with its sister city, Belfast (10 to 12 hours, £20). From North Wales, boats sail from Holyhead to Dun Laoghaire (pronounced "dunleary") three or four times a day (£18-£25, 3½ hours, get ticket ASAP in London, special deal for car plus five passengers for around £120). Prices on planes, trains, buses and boats vary with the season. Round-trips, Monday-Thursday departures, stays over a Saturday, and tickets bought 7 days in advance are usually cheaper. The London-Dublin 10-hour train/boat ride costs about £50, overnight or all day. The London-Dublin 12-hour bus trip costs £32 one-way or round-trip. Flights from London to Dublin and Belfast are fairly cheap (£95 regular one-way, £60 round-trip when purchased a week in advance and staying over Saturday, £34 one-way for those under 26) and easy to arrange at a London travel agency. Consider an "open-jaws" flight plan, flying into London and home from Ireland. Your 22-day itinerary would then be: London, Wales, England, Scotland, Belfast, Dublin, West Ireland, home.

If you'll be touring the Continent with a Eurailpass, start it in Ireland (it's good on Irish trains and many buses) and ride free on the otherwise-expensive 24-hour boat ride to France.

Transportation in Ireland: Irish trains are expensive and not extensive, with meager schedules and coverage. BritRail passes don't work here. The bus is cheaper and has more extensive routes. Consider special bus passes. Students get a 50 percent discount with ISIC cards. Taking a car from England is complicated and expensive. Most people make arrangements from the U.S.A. to rent a car (by the week). Many hitchhikers find Ireland easy to get around in, safe, and very friendly.

Ireland Extension

Revise your 22-day plan to end in Edinburgh. Turn in car in Edinburgh if driving. Then start on this 7-day trip through Ireland.

Suggested Itinerary
Day 1 Edinburgh-Glasgow-bus/boat-Belfast.
Day 2 Sightsee in Belfast, afternoon at Cultra Folk Museum.
Day 3 Early train to Dublin, sightsee all day.
Day 4 Dublin.
Day 5 Dublin-Cashel-Tralee-Dingle.
Day 6 Dingle, bike the peninsula.
Day 7 Dingle-Tralee-Shannon Airport to fly home; or Dingle-Dublin and night train/boat to London.

Sightseeing Highlights

Dublin—Dublin, worth a day or two, crowds around O'Connell Street Bridge and the River Liffey. Boats land at nearby Dun Laoghaire with good bus connections into Dublin. (TI, 8:30 a.m.-6:00 p.m., closed Sunday, has a room-finding service, 14 Upper O'Connell Street, tel. 1/8747733.)

Orient yourself by taking a city walking tour (ask at the TI). Visit Trinity College (stately grounds, historic buildings, illuminated Book of Kells manuscript); the National Museum (moving Nathan Hale-type patriotism of the martyrs of the 1916 Rebellion, impressive medieval and earlier Irish artifacts); and Kilmainham Jail (symbol of the Irish struggle against Britain, martyr memorabilia). For something entirely different, tour the Guinness Brewery (Monday-Friday 10:00 a.m.-5:00 p.m., video show, free beer).

For entertainment, sample the great Irish theater (Abbey Theater and many others, shows Monday-Saturday, 8:00 p.m.), seek out some Irish folk music in a local pub, or check out Irish sports—hurling (the rugged national sport that's like airborne hockey with no injury time-outs) or Gaelic football (a violent form of rugby). Games are held nearly every Sunday at Dublin's Croke Park. Use the periodical entertainment guide called *In Dublin* for music, theater, sports, and tour listings.

Glendalough—The best short day-trip from Dublin for a sample of rural Ireland is a visit to Glendalough in the Wicklow mountains. Fifteen hundred years ago, the hermit St. Kevin established a thriving monastic school here.

Today its ruins, surrounded by scenic forests and lakes, are understandably popular with tourists. Look into a 1-day tour from Dublin.

Belfast—A direct 3-hour train ride north of Dublin, the capital of the North offers a safe, fascinating look at "The Troubles." Passing the check-point, you'll step into the traffic-free "safe zone." Browse through a bomb-damage clearance sale. Take a side trip south to the wonderful Cultra Open-Air Folk Museum; talk to the people. Check out the positive and creative way Belfast is splicing together their Protestant and Catholic young people. By riding a shared taxi up Falls Road into a working-class Catholic neighborhood, you can get a look at some powerful mural art and visit the national cemetery. With a little common sense (don't sing Catholic songs in Protestant pubs), Belfast is as safe as London. (See the chapter on Belfast in my book, *Europe Through the Back Door*.) Belfast-Glasgow bus connections are great.

Cork—Ireland's rough, but pleasant, second city, is visited mostly for the nearby Blarney Castle with its too-famous Blarney Stone. Hordes of visiting Americans smother it with kisses to get the "gift of gab"; local guys pee on it to get the gift of hilarity.

Cashel—This stirring religious and political center dates back to the mysterious days of St. Patrick. Fine Celtic cross graveyard, good tours (two buses daily from Dublin and Cork).

Dingle Peninsula—My favorite scenery in the British Isles is Ireland's West Coast, and the best in the west is the rugged beauty of hearty Dingle Peninsula, just north of the very touristy Ring of Kerry. Dingle is a Gaeltacht—a region where the locals still speak the old Irish or Gaelic language. This is a cultural preserve with traditional dress, music, and lifestyles complementing the natural beauty. (See the *Europe Through the Back Door* chapter on Dingle.) Train to the pleasant town of Tralee, then bus or thumb to Dingle town. Set up at Mrs. Farrell's Corner House (S-£13, D-£26, Dykegate Street, tel. 066/51516) or Paddy Fenton's Ballintaggert House Hostel (£6 beds, tel. 066/51454) on the Tralee road just east of town. Rent a bike for the circular trip out to Slea Head (closest point to the USA, incredible scenery, villages; explore the medieval monks' stone beehive huts, or *clochans*, along the way), but be home in time to catch the nightly folk music at O'Flaherty's Pub. **Moran's Slea Head Tours** are the best way to explore Dingle peninsula without your own car. John Moran mini-buses small groups for 3 hours (£6, 2:15 p.m., not Sunday, many morning departures in July and August, tel. 066/51155, fax 51553).

Galway—The largest city in western Ireland, coastal Galway is cozy, historic, and 3 hours by train from Dublin and Cork (direct bus service to Rosslare, a ferry port). Daily boats and cheap flights to the Aran Islands.

Aran Islands—Off the coast of Galway, this tiny group of wave-whipped islands is a stark, stubborn outpost of old Irish culture and not terribly touristy. Spend a day on the main island, rent a bike, and explore. Boats connect islands with the mainland. One goes to Doolin, home of Ireland's best folk music, but not much else.

Donegal—Ireland in the extreme, Donegal is the cultural Yukon of this lush island, where everyone seems to be typecast for an Irish movie. Enter Donegal with caution, for while it has no real "sights," it is seductive, and many unwary visitors end up skipping the rest of their itinerary.

Helpful Hints

Understand Ireland's "Troubles"—the North-South, Catholic-Protestant problem. A fine background and wonderful reading is *Trinity* by Leon Uris.

Ireland is small, about 150 miles by 200 miles, but it has no English-style motorways. Transportation is slow. Approach every trip as a joyride. Traveling in Ireland is generally cheaper than in England. The Irish pound is worth a little less than the British pound.

Ireland's B&Bs are even cozier and less expensive than England's, and traveling without reservations is not difficult. Use the *Let's Go: Britain and Ireland* guidebook. Ireland's weather ranges from damp to drizzly to downpour, and her people are her main attraction. You can't enjoy Ireland without enjoying her people.

GREAT BRITAIN BY TRAIN AND BUS

Britain has a great train and bus system, and travelers who don't want to (or can't afford to) drive a rental car can enjoy 22 exciting days using public transportation.

Deals on Wheels

Regular tickets on Britain's great train system (15,000 departures from 2,400 stations daily) are the most expensive per mile in all of Europe. Those who go round-trip, buy in advance, or ride the bus save big. For instance, the regular fare for the 2-hour train trip from York to London is £44 ($70). The **APEX** fare is only £33 (book 7 days in advance) and the **SuperSaver** fare is £45 round-trip (no advance booking necessary, but no travel allowed on Friday or during morning rush hour, open return). The bus makes the trip from York to London in 4 hours for about £35. Round-trip bus tickets usually cost the same as one-way fares.

The pattern is clear and consistent: trains are twice as fast and 50 percent more expensive than buses. But buses go many places that trains don't.

Railpasses can be a good deal. The BritRail pass comes in "consecutive day" and "flexi" versions, with price breaks for second class, youths, and seniors. (I see no reason to pay extra for first class.) BritRail passes cover England, Scotland, and Wales. There are now Scotland passes, England/Wales passes, and a new BritIreland pass. While there are several "BritRail Drive" passes, which allow you

BritRail Pass Rates 1994					Flexipass	
	8 days	15 days	22 days	1 month	4 in 8	8 in 15
Youth (under 26)	179	269	339	395	155	219
Economy	219	339	425	495	189	269
First Class	299	489	645	775	249	389
Senior Economy (over 60)	199	305	379	445	169	245

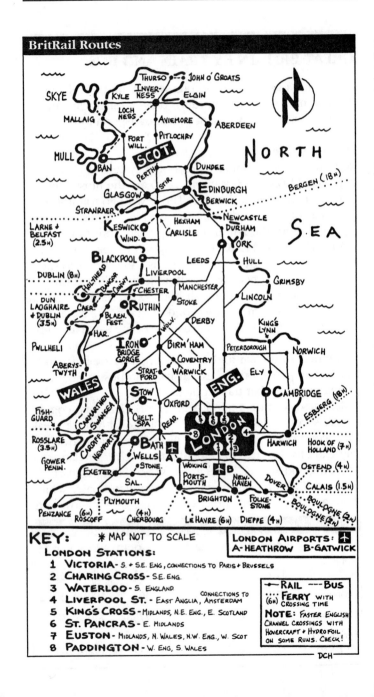

BritRail Routes

KEY: ✱ MAP NOT TO SCALE

LONDON STATIONS:

1. **VICTORIA** - S. + S.E. ENG, CONNECTIONS TO PARIS + BRUSSELS
2. **CHARING CROSS** - S.E. ENG.
3. **WATERLOO** - S. ENGLAND
4. **LIVERPOOL ST.** - East Anglia, Amsterdam CONNECTIONS TO
5. **KING'S CROSS** - MIDLANDS, N.E. ENG., E. SCOTLAND
6. **ST. PANCRAS** - E. MIDLANDS
7. **EUSTON** - MIDLANDS, N. WALES, N.W. ENG., W. SCOT
8. **PADDINGTON** - W. ENG, S. WALES

LONDON AIRPORTS: ✈
A - HEATHROW   B - GATWICK

•—•— RAIL   --- BUS
⋯⋯ FERRY WITH
(6H) CROSSING TIME
NOTE: FASTER ENGLISH
CHANNEL CROSSINGS WITH
HOVERCRAFT + HYDROFOIL
ON SOME RUNS. CHECK!

DCH

to take a day of rail here and a day of car rental there, since they jump from 15 days to 30 days, they don't fit this plan economically. These passes are sold outside of Europe only. For specifics, contact your travel agent, or Europe Through the Back Door (tel. 206-771-8303).

Budget travelers can save a wad with a bus pass. These are sold in the USA (1-800-327-6097) for 20 percent more than the price you'd pay in Britain. The National Express sells the following Tourist Trail bus passes (over the counter): 5 days (£65), 8 days (£90), 15 days (£135), 22 days (£160), 30 days (£190). Those over age 59 and under 24 save 33 percent. Bus stations are normally at or near train stations. The British distinguish between "buses" (for local runs with lots of stops) and "coaches" (long distance, express runs).

Connecting London with Europe

While it's hard to nail down exact prices and options for those traveling from London to Paris or Amsterdam, it's safe to say that these routes are very competitive and you'll get better prices in London than from the USA. Taking the bus is cheapest. Round-trips are a bargain. Flying is more reasonable than you might expect. Students get great deals.

London to Paris—By bus: £33 one-way, £55 round-trip within 6 months, 10 hours, day or overnight, on Eurolines (tel. 071/730-8235) or CitySprint (tel. 0304/240241). By train: £42 one-way overnight, £57 by day, 7 hours, £65 round-trip within 5 days, £85 round-trip within 2 months. BritRail Hover Speed crossing in 6 hours for £60. By plane: £90 regular, £40 student stand-by.

London to Amsterdam—By bus: £32 one-way, 12 hours, day or night, £53 round-trip within 6 months, Eurolines, same price to Brussels. By train: £50 one-way, day or night, 12 hours, £63 round-trip within 5 days, £83 round-trip within 2 months. To fly: £92 regular.

WHAT'S SO GREAT ABOUT BRITAIN?

Regardless of the revolution we had 200 years ago, Americans "go home" to Britain. This most popular tourist destination has a strange influence and power over us.

Britain is small—about the size of Uganda (or Idaho)—600 miles tall and 300 miles at its widest. Its highest mountain is 4,400 feet—a foothill by our standards. The population is a quarter of the U.S.A.'s. Politically and economically, Great Britain is closing out the twentieth century only a weak shadow of the days when it boasted, "The sun never sets on the British Empire."

At one time, Britain owned one-fifth of the world and accounted for more than half the planet's industrial output. Today, the Empire is down to tidbits such as the Falklands and Northern Ireland, Great Britain's industrial production is about 5 percent of the world's total, and Italy has a higher per capita income.

Still, Britain is a world leader. Her heritage, her culture, and her people cannot be measured in traditional units of power. The United Kingdom is a union of four countries—England, Wales, Scotland, and Northern Ireland. Cynics call it an English Empire ruled by London, and there is some tension between the dominant Anglo-Saxon English (46 million) and their Celtic brothers (10 million).

In the Dark Ages, the Angles moved into this region from Europe, pushing the Celtic inhabitants to the undesirable fringe of the islands. The Angles settled in Angleland (England), while the Celts made do in Wales, Scotland, and Ireland.

Today, Wales, with 2 million people, struggles along with a terrible economy, dragged down by the depressed mining industry. A great deal of Welsh pride is apparent in the local music and the bilingual signs—some with the English spray-painted out. Fifty thousand people speak Welsh.

Scotland is big, accounting for one-third of Great Britain's land area, but sparsely inhabited, with only 5 million people. Only about 80,000 speak Gaelic, but the Scots enjoy a large measure of autonomy with their separate Church of Scotland, their own legal system, and Scottish currency (essentially interchangeable with the British).

Ireland is divided. Most of it is the completely independent and Catholic Republic of Ireland. The top quarter is Northern Ireland—ruled from London. Long ago, the

Protestant English and Scots moved into the north, the (most Catholic and) industrial heartland of Ireland, and told the Catholic Irish to "go to Hell or go to Connemara." The Irish moved to the bleak and less productive parts of the island, like Connemara, and the seeds of today's "Troubles" were planted. There's no easy answer or easy blame, but the island has struggled—its population is only one-third (3 million) of what it used to be—and the battle continues.

As a visitor today, you'll see a politically polarized England. The Conservatives, proponents of Victorian values—community, family, hard work, thrift, and trickle-down economics—are taking a Reaganesque approach to Britain's serious problems. The Labor and Liberal parties see an almost irreparable break-up of the social service programs so dear to them and so despised by those with much to conserve.

Basic British History for the Traveler

When Julius Caesar landed on the misty and mysterious isle of Britain in 55 B.C., England entered the history books. The primitive Celtic tribes he conquered were themselves invaders, who had earlier conquered the even more mysterious people who built Stonehenge long before.

The Romans built towns and roads and established their capital at "Londinium." The Celtic natives, consisting of Gaels, Picts, and Scots, were not subdued so easily in Scotland and Wales, so the Romans built Hadrian's Wall near the Scottish border to keep invading Scots out. Even today, the Celtic language and influence are strongest in these far reaches of Britain. As Rome fell, so fell Roman Britain—a victim of invaders and internal troubles. Barbarian tribes from Germany and Denmark called Angles and Saxons swept through the southern part of the island, establishing Angle-land. These were the days of the real King Arthur, possibly a Christianized Roman general fighting valiantly, but in vain, against invading barbarians. The island was plunged into 500 years of Dark Ages—wars, plagues, and poverty—lit only by the dim candle of a few learned Christian monks and missionaries trying to convert the barbarians.

Modern England began with yet another invasion. William the Conqueror and his Norman troops crossed the channel from France in 1066. William crowned himself king in Westminster Abbey (where all subsequent coronations would take place) and began building the Tower of London. French-speaking Norman kings ruled the country for two centuries. Then the country suffered through two centuries of civil wars, with various noble families vying for the crown. In one of the most bitter feuds, the York and Lancaster families fought the War of the Roses, so-called because of the white and red flowers the combatants chose as their symbols. Battles; intrigues; kings, nobles, and ladies imprisoned and executed in the Tower—it's a wonder the country survived its rulers.

England was finally united by the "third-party" Tudor family. Henry VIII, a Tudor, was England's Renaissance king. He was handsome, athletic, a poet, a scholar, and a musician. He was also arrogant, cruel, gluttonous, and paranoid. He went through six wives in forty years, divorcing, imprisoning, or beheading them when they no longer suited his needs. Henry "divorced" England from the Catholic Church, establishing the Protestant Church of England (Anglican Church) and setting in motion years of religious squabbles. He also "dissolved" the monasteries, leaving just the shells of many formerly glorious abbeys dotting the countryside.

Henry's daughter, Queen Elizabeth I, made England a great naval and trading power and presided over the Elizabethan era of great writers, including Shakespeare.

The long-standing quarrel between England's "divine right" kings and nobles in Parliament finally erupted into a Civil War (1643). Parliament forces under the Puritan farmer Oliver Cromwell defeated—and beheaded—King Charles I. This Civil War left its mark on much of what you'll see in England. Eventually, Parliament invited Charles's son to retake the throne. This restoration of the monarchy was accompanied by a great rebuilding of London (including Christopher Wren's St. Paul's

Cathedral), which had been devastated by the Great Fire of 1666.

Britain grew as a great naval power, colonizing and trading with all parts of the globe. Her naval superiority ("Britannia rules the waves") was secured by Admiral Nelson's victory over Napoleon's fleet at the Battle of Trafalgar, while Lord Wellington stomped Napoleon on land at Waterloo. Nelson and Wellington are memorialized by many arches, columns, and squares throughout England.

Economically, Britain led the world into the Industrial Age with her mills, factories, coal mines, and trains. By the time of Queen Victoria's reign (1837-1901), Britain was at the zenith of power with a colonial empire that covered one-fifth of the world. The twentieth century has not been kind to Britain, however. Two World Wars devastated the population. The Nazi Blitz reduced much of London to rubble. Her colonial empire has dwindled to almost nothing, and she is no longer an economic superpower. The "Irish Troubles" are a constant thorn as the Catholic inhabitants of British-ruled Northern Ireland fight for the same independence their southern neighbors won decades ago. The war over the Falkland Islands in 1982 showed how little of the British Empire is left, but also how determined the British are to hang onto what remains.

But the tradition (if not the substance) of greatness continues, presided over by Queen Elizabeth II, her husband Prince Phillip, the heir-apparent Prince Charles, and a distant relative—his wife, Princess Diana. With economic problems, the separation of Charles and Diana, the Fergie fiasco, and a relentless popular press, the royal family is having a tough time. But the queen has stayed above the mess and most British people still jump at an opportunity to see royalty. American on-lookers should remember that royal marriages have historically been disasters. The problems of Charles and Diana seem unprecedented only because they follow the unusually happy married lives of Queen Elizabeth and her mother. Britain remains a constitutional monarchy.

Britain's Royal Families

800-1066	Saxon and Danish kings
1066-1150	Norman invasion, Norman kings
1150-1400	Plantagenets
1400-1460	Lancaster
1460-1485	York
1485-1600	Tudor (Henry VIII, Elizabeth I)
1600-1649	Stuart (with civil war and beheading of Charles I)
1649-1660	Commonwealth, Cromwell, no royal head of state
1660-1700	Stuart restoration of monarchy
1700-1900	Hanover (4 Georges, Victoria)
1900-1910	Edward VII
1910-	House of Windsor (George V, Edward VII, George VI, Elizabeth II)

Architecture in Britain

From Stonehenge to Big Ben, travelers are storming castle walls, climbing spiral staircases, and snapping the pictures of 5,000 years of architecture. Let's sort it out.

The oldest stuff—mysterious and prehistoric—goes from before Roman times back to 3000 B.C. The earliest—such as Stonehenge and Avebury—is from the Stone and Bronze Ages. The remains from this period are made of huge stones or mounds of earth, even manmade hills, and were built as celestial calendars and for worship or burial. Iron Age people (600 B.C. to A.D. 43) left us desolate stone forts. The Romans thrived in Britain from A.D. 50 to 400, building cities, walls, and roads. Evidence of Roman greatness can be seen in lavish villas with ornate mosaic floors, temples uncovered beneath great English churches, and Roman stones in medieval city walls. Roman roads sliced across the island in straight lines. Today, unusually straight rural roads are very likely laid directly on ancient Roman roads.

Roman Britain crumbled in the fifth century, and there was little building in Dark Age (Anglo-Saxon) England. Architecturally, the light was switched on with the Norman Conquest in 1066. As William earned his title "the

Conqueror," he built churches and castles in the European Romanesque style.

English Romanesque is called "Norman" (1066-1200). Norman churches had round arches, thick walls, and small windows. Durham Cathedral and the Chapel of St. John in the Tower of London are typical Norman churches. The Tower of London, with its square keep, small windows, and spiral stone stairways, is a typical Norman castle. You'll see plenty of Norman castles—all built to secure the conquest of these invaders from Normandy.

Gothic architecture (1200-1600) replaced the heavy Norman style with light, vertical buildings, pointed arches, tall soaring spires, and bigger windows. English Gothic is divided into three stages. Early English (1200-1300) features tall, simple spires, beautifully carved capitals, and elaborate chapter houses (such as the Wells cathedral). Decorated Gothic (1300-1370) gets fancier with more elaborate tracery, bigger windows, and ornately carved pinnacles, as you'll see at Westminster Abbey. Finally, the perpendicular style (1370-1600) goes back to square towers and emphasizes straight, uninterrupted vertical lines from ceiling to floor with vast windows and exuberant decoration including fan-vaulted ceilings (King's College Chapel at Cambridge).

As you tour the great medieval churches of England, remember, nearly everything is symbolic. Local guides and books help us modern pilgrims understand at least a little of what we see. For instance, on the tombs, if the figure has crossed legs, he was a crusader. If his feet rest on a dog, he died at home, but if the legs rest on a lion, he died in battle.

Wales is particularly rich in English castles, needed to subdue the stubborn Welsh. Edward I built a ring of powerful castles in Wales (such as Caernarfon and Conway).

Gothic houses were a simple mix of woven strips of thin wood, rubble, and plaster called wattle and daub. The famous black-and-white Tudor, or half-timbered, look came simply from filling in heavy oak frames with wattle and daub.

The Tudor period (1485-1560) was a time of relative peace (the War of the Roses was finally over), prosperity, and renaissance. Henry VIII broke with the Catholic church and "dissolved" (destroyed) the monasteries, leaving scores of England's greatest churches gutted shells. These hauntingly beautiful abbey ruins surrounded by lush lawns (Glastonbury, Tintern, Whitby) are now pleasant city parks. York's magnificent Minster survived only because Henry needed an administrative headquarters in the North for his Anglican church.

Although few churches were built, this was a time of house and mansion construction. Warmth was becoming popular and affordable, and Tudor buildings featured small square windows and often many chimneys. In towns where land was scarce, many Tudor houses grew up and out, getting wider with each overhanging floor.

The Elizabethan and Jacobean periods (1560-1620) were followed by the English Renaissance style (1620-1720). English architects mixed Gothic and classical styles, then baroque and classical styles. Although the ornate baroque never really grabbed England, the classical style of the Italian architect Palladio did. Inigo Jones (1573-1652), Christopher Wren (1632-1723), and those they inspired plastered England with enough columns, domes, and symmetry to please a Caesar. The Great Fire of London (1666) cleared the way for an ambitious young Wren to put his mark on London forever with a grand rebuilding scheme, including the great St. Paul's and more than fifty other churches.

The Georgian period (1720-1840), featuring the lousy German kings of England whom the celebrants of the Boston Tea Party couldn't stand, was rich and showed off by being very classical. Grand pedimental doorways, fine cast-ironwork on balconies and railings, Chippendale furniture, and white-on-blue Wedgewood ceramics graced rich homes everywhere. John Wood, Jr. and Sr., led the way, giving the trend-setting city of Bath its crescents and circles of aristocratic Georgian rowhouses.

The Industrial Revolution shaped the Victorian period (1840-1890) with glass, steel, and iron. England had a huge new erector set (so did France's Mr. Eiffel). This was also a romantic period, reviving the "more Christian" Gothic style. London's Houses of Parliament are neo-Gothic—just 100 years old but looking 700, except for the tell-tale modern precision and craftsmanship. Whereas Gothic was stone or concrete, neo-Gothic was often red brick. These were England's glory days, and there was more building in this period than in all previous ages combined.

The architecture of our century obeys the formula "form follows function"—it works well but isn't particularly interesting. England treasures its heritage and takes great pains to build tastefully in historic districts and to preserve its many "listed" buildings. With a booming tourist trade, these quaint reminders of its—and our—past are becoming a valuable part of the British economy.

British TV

British television is so good—and so British—that it deserves a mention as a sightseeing treat. After a hard day of castle-climbing, watch the telly over a pot of tea in the comfortable living room of your village bed and breakfast.

England has four channels. BBC 1 and BBC 2 are government regulated, commercial-free, and rather high-brow. ITV and Channel 4 are private, a little more Yankee, and have commercials—but those commercials are clever, sophisticated, and a fun look at England. Broadcasting is funded by a £70-per-year-per-household tax. Hmmm, 35 cents per day to escape commercials. Whereas California "accents" fill our airwaves 24 hours a day, homogenizing the way our country speaks, England protects and promotes its regional accents by its choice of TV and radio announcers. Commercial-free British TV is looser than it used to be, but is still careful about what it airs and when.

American shows are very popular—especially *Quantum Leap*. Oldies such as *Cheers* and *All in the Family* are also broadcasted. The visiting viewer should be sure to tune in a few typical English shows. I'd recommend a dose of English situation and political comedy fun (*Spitting Image*) and the top-notch BBC evening news. For a tear-filled taste of British soap, see the popular *Coronation Street* or *Eastenders*, and for an English Johnny Carson, see Noel Edmond's comedy show.

And, of course, if you like the crazy, offbeat Benny Hill and Monty Python-type comedy, you've come to the right place.

TELEPHONE DIRECTORY

City	Area Code/ Tourist Info	Train Info
London	no TI phone	928-5100
Salisbury	0722/334956	27591
Bath	0225/462831	0272/294255
Wells	0749/672552	
Cardiff	0222/227281	228000
Stow-on-the-Wold	0451/831082	0452/529501
Chipping Campden	0386/840101	
Stratford	0789/293127	091/22302
Coventry	0203/832303	555211
Ironbridge Gorge	0952/432166	
Ruthin, N. Wales	0824/703992	
Blackpool	0253/21623	20375
Windermere	05394/46499	
Keswick	07687/72645	0228/44711
Oban	0631/63122	63083
Inverness	0463/234353	238924
Edinburgh	031/557-1700	556-2451
Hadrian's Wall	0434/605225	
Durham	091/384-3720	232-6262
York	0904/621756	642155
Cambridge	0223/322640	311999
Dublin	01/8747733	366222

Other useful numbers

Emergency	999
Operator	100
Dir. Assist. Outside London	192
London Dir. Assist.	142
U.S. Embassy	071/499/9000
Internat'l information	155
Lake District weather report	09662/45151

London airports and airlines

Heathrow
General Information: 081/759-4321, Terminal 3: 081/745-7412, Terminal 4: 081/745-4540, Air Canada: 081/897-1331 American: 081/572-5555, British Air: 081/759-2525, SAS: 0426/931-301, United Airlines: 0426/915-500, TWA: 081/579-5352.

Gatwick
General Information: 0293/531-299, American, Dan Air, Delta, Northwest, and USAir: all 0293/567-955, TWA: 0293/567-711.

International code 010

U.S.A.	1	Germany	49
Canada	1	Italy	39
Belgium	32	Netherlands	31
France	33	Switzerland	41
Ireland	353		

AT&T "U.S.A. direct": 0800-8900-11
MCI "U.S.A. direct": 0800-89-02-22
SPRINT "U.S.A. direct": 0800-89-0877
"Canada Direct": 0800-89-0016

WEIGHTS AND MEASURES

1 imperial gallon = 1.2 U.S. gallons or about 5 liters
1 stone = 14 lbs. (a 175 lb. person weighs 12 stone)
British pint = 1.2 U.S. pints
1 mile = 1.6 kilometers. 1 kilometer = 6/10 mile
Shoe sizes—about ½ to 1½ sizes smaller than in U.S.

BRITISH-YANKEE VOCABULARY

British/American
banger   sausage
bap   hamburger-type bun
biscuit   cookie
bloke   man, guy
bonnet   car hood
boot   car trunk
brilliant   cool
candy floss   cotton candy
cheers   goodbye or thanks
chemist   pharmacy
chips   French fries
concession   discounted admission
crisps   potato chips
dicey   iffy, questionable
dinner   lunch
dual carriageway   four-lane highway
fag   cigarette
faggot   meatball
first floor   second floor
fortnight   two weeks
give way   yield
half eight   8:30 (not 7:30)
hoover   vacuum cleaner
iced lolly   popsicle
interval   intermission at the theater
ironmonger   hardware store
jumble   sale, rummage sale
jumper   sweater
knickers   underpants
knock up   wake up or visit
loo   bathroom
lorry   truck
motorway   highway
nackered   dead tired
nosh   food
off license   can sell take-away liquor
take away   to go

petrol   gas
pillar box   postbox
queue up   line up
randy   horny
ring up   call (telephone)
rubber   eraser
self-catering   accommodation with kitchen facilities
                    rented by the week
serviette   napkin
single ticket   one-way ticket
solicitor   lawyer
stone   14 lbs. weight
subway   underground pedestrian passageway
sweets   candy
telly   TV
to let   for rent
torch   flashlight
trunk call   long distance phone call
underground   subway
verge   edge of road
wellingtons, wellies   rubber boots
zebra crossing   crosswalk
zed   the letter "z"

INDEX

Rick Steves'

EUROPE THROUGH THE BACK DOOR CATALOG

All items are field tested, discount priced (prices include tax and shipping), completely guaranteed, and highly recommended for European travel.

CONVERTIBLE BACK DOOR BAG $75

At 9"x21"x13" our specially designed, sturdy bag is maximum carry-on-the-plane size (fits under the seat) and your key to footloose and fancy-free travel. Made of rugged water resistant cordura nylon, it converts easily from a smart looking suitcase to a handy rucksack. It has padded hide-away shoulder straps, top and side handles, and a detachable shoulder strap (for use as a suitcase). Lockable perimeter zippers allow easy access to the roomy 2,500 cubic inch central compartment. Two large outside compartments are perfect for frequently used items. A nylon stuff bag is also included. Rick Steves and over 40,000 other Back Door travelers have lived out of these bags all around the world. Available in black, grey, navy blue and teal green.

MONEYBELT $8

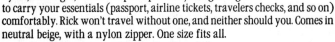

Absolutely required for European travel, our sturdy nylon, ultra-light, under-the-pants pouch is just big enough to carry your essentials (passport, airline tickets, travelers checks, and so on) comfortably. Rick won't travel without one, and neither should you. Comes in neutral beige, with a nylon zipper. One size fits all.

EUROPEAN RAILPASSES

We sell the full range of European railpasses, and with every Eurailpass we give you these important extras -- *free:* Rick Steves' 90-minute "How to get the most out of your railpass" video; your choice of one of Rick's seven "2 to 22 Days in..." guidebooks; and our comments on your 1-page proposed itinerary. Call us for a free copy of our 48-page *1994 Back Door Guide to European Railpasses.*

BACK DOOR 'BEST OF EUROPE' TOURS

We offer a variety of European tours for those who want to travel in the Back Door style, but without the transportation and hotel hassles. These tours feature small groups, our own guides, Back Door accomodations, and lots of physical exercise. Our tours aren't for everyone, but they may be just the ticket for you. Call us for details.

FREE TRAVEL NEWSLETTER/CATALOG

Give us a call at (206) 771-8303, and we'll send you our free newsletter/catalog packed full of info on budget travel, books, maps, videos railpasses and tours. We'll help you travel better *because* you're on a budget -- not in spite of it.

Prices are good through 1994 (maybe longer), and include tax and shipping (allow 2 to 3 weeks). Sorry, no credit cards or phone orders. Send checks in US $ to:

Europe Through the Back Door ❖ 109 Fourth Avenue North PO Box 2009, Edmonds, WA 98020 ❖ Phone: (206)771-8303

Other Books from John Muir Publications

Asia Through the Back Door, 4th ed., 400 pp. $16.95 (available 7/93)

Belize: A Natural Destination, 336 pp. $16.95

Costa Rica: A Natural Destination, 2nd ed., 310 pp. $16.95

Elderhostels: The Students' Choice, 2nd ed., 304 pp. $15.95

Environmental Vacations: Volunteer Projects to Save the Planet, 2nd ed., 248 pp. $16.95

Europe 101: History & Art for the Traveler, 4th ed., 350 pp. $15.95

Europe Through the Back Door, 11th ed., 432 pp. $17.95

Europe Through the Back Door Phrase Book: French, 160 pp. $4.95

Europe Through the Back Door Phrase Book: German, 160 pp. $4.95

Europe Through the Back Door Phrase Book: Italian, 168 pp. $4.95

Europe Through the Back Door Phrase Book: Spanish & Portuguese, 288 pp. $4.95

A Foreign Visitor's Guide to America, 224 pp. $12.95

Great Cities of Eastern Europe, 256 pp. $16.95

Guatemala: A Natural Destination, 336 pp. $16.95

Indian America: A Traveler's Companion, 4th ed., 448 pp. $17.95 (available 7/93)

Interior Furnishings Southwest, 256 pp. $19.95

Mona Winks: Self-Guided Tours of Europe's Top Museums, 2nd ed., 448 pp. $16.95

Opera! The Guide to Western Europe's Great Houses, 296 pp. $18.95

Paintbrushes and Pistols: How the Taos Artists Sold the West, 288 pp. $17.95

The People's Guide to Mexico, 9th ed., 608 pp. $18.95

Ranch Vacations: The Complete Guide to Guest and Resort, Fly-Fishing, and Cross-Country Skiing Ranches, 2nd ed., 396 pp. $18.95

The Shopper's Guide to Art and Crafts in the Hawaiian Islands, 272 pp. $13.95

The Shopper's Guide to Mexico, 224 pp. $9.95

Understanding Europeans, 272 pp. $14.95

Undiscovered Islands of the Caribbean, 3rd ed., 288 pp. $14.95

Undiscovered Islands of the Mediterranean, 2nd ed., 224 pp. $13.95

Undiscovered Islands of the U.S. and Canadian West Coast, 288 pp. $12.95

Unique Colorado, 112 pp. $10.95 (available 6/93)

Unique Florida, 112 pp. $10.95 (available 7/93)

Unique New Mexico, 112 pp. $10.95 (available 6/93)

A Viewer's Guide to Art: A Glossary of Gods, People, and Creatures, 144 pp. $10.95

The Visitor's Guide to the Birds of the Eastern National Parks: United States and Canada, 410 pp. $15.95

2 to 22 Days Series
Each title offers 22 flexible daily itineraries useful for planning vacations of any length. Aside from valuable general information, included are "must see" attractions *and* hidden "jewels."

2 to 22 Days in the American Southwest, 1993 ed., 176 pp. $10.95

2 to 22 Days in Asia, 1993 ed., 176 pp. $9.95

2 to 22 Days in Australia, 1993 ed., 192 pp. $9.95

2 to 22 Days in California, 1993 ed., 192 pp. $9.95
2 to 22 Days in Europe, 1993 ed., 288 pp. $13.95
2 to 22 Days in Florida, 1993 ed., 192 pp. $10.95
2 to 22 Days in France, 1993 ed., 192 pp. $10.95
2 to 22 Days in Germany, Austria, & Switzerland, 1993 ed., 224 pp. $10.95
2 to 22 Days in Great Britain, 1993 ed., 192 pp. $10.95
2 to 22 Days Around the Great Lakes, 1993 ed., 192 pp. $10.95
2 to 22 Days in Hawaii, 1993 ed., 192 pp. $9.95
2 to 22 Days in Italy, 208 pp. $10.95
2 to 22 Days in New England, 1993 ed., 192 pp. $10.95
2 to 22 Days in New Zealand, 1993 ed., 192 pp. $9.95
2 to 22 Days in Norway, Sweden, & Denmark, 1993 ed., 192 pp. $10.95
2 to 22 Days in the Pacific Northwest, 1993 ed., 192 pp. $10.95
2 to 22 Days in the Rockies, 1993 ed., 192 pp. $10.95
2 to 22 Days in Spain & Portugal, 192 pp. $10.95
2 to 22 Days in Texas, 1993 ed., 192 pp. $9.95
2 to 22 Days in Thailand, 1993 ed., 180 pp. $9.95
22 Days (or More) Around the World, 1993 ed., 264 pp. $12.95

Automotive Titles
How to Keep Your VW Alive, 15th ed., 464 pp. $21.95
How to Keep Your Subaru Alive 480 pp. $21.95
How to Keep Your Toyota Pickup Alive 392 pp. $21.95
How to Keep Your Datsun/Nissan Alive 544 pp. $21.95
The Greaseless Guide to Car Care Confidence, 224 pp. $14.95
Off-Road Emergency Repair & Survival, 160 pp. $9.95

TITLES FOR YOUNG READERS AGES 8 AND UP
"Kidding Around" Travel Guides for Young Readers
All the "Kidding Around" Travel guides are 64 pages and $9.95 paper,
except for **Kidding Around Spain** and **Kidding Around the National
Parks of the Southwest,** which are 108 pages and $12.95 paper.
Kidding Around Atlanta
Kidding Around Boston,2nd ed.
Kidding Around Chicago, 2nd ed.
Kidding Around the Hawaiian Islands
Kidding Around London
Kidding Around Los Angeles
Kidding Around the National Parks of the Southwest
Kidding Around New York City, 2nd ed.
Kidding Around Paris
Kidding Around Philadelphia
Kidding Around San Diego
Kidding Around San Francisco
Kidding Around Santa Fe
Kidding Around Seattle
Kidding Around Spain
Kidding Around Washington, D.C., 2nd ed.

"Extremely Weird" Series for Young Readers. Written by Sarah
Lovett, each is 48 pages and $9.95 paper.
Extremely Weird Bats
Extremely Weird Birds
Extremely Weird Endangered Species
Extremely Weird Fishes
Extremely Weird Frogs

Extremely Weird Insects
Extremely Weird Mammals (available 8/93)
Extremely Weird Micro Monsters (available 8/93)
Extremely Weird Primates
Extremely Weird Reptiles
Extremely Weird Sea Creatures
Extremely Weird Snakes (available 8/93)
Extremely Weird Spiders

"Masters of Motion" Series for Young Readers. Each title is 48 pages and $9.95 paper.
How to Drive an Indy Race Car
How to Fly a 747
How to Fly the Space Shuttle

"X-ray Vision" Series for Young Readers. Each title is 48 pages and $9.95 paper.
Looking Inside Cartoon Animation
Looking Inside Sports Aerodynamics
Looking Inside the Brain
Looking Inside Sunken Treasure
Looking Inside Telescopes and the Night Sky

Multicultural Titles for Young Readers
Native Artists of North America, 48 pp. $14.95 hardcover
The Indian Way: Learning to Communicate with Mother Earth,
114 pp. $9.95
The Kids' Environment Book: What's Awry and Why, 192 pp. $13.95
Kids Explore America's African-American Heritage, 112 pp. $8.95
Kids Explore America's Hispanic Heritage, 112 pp. $7.95

Environmental Titles for Young Readers
Rads, Ergs, and Cheeseburgers: The Kids' Guide to Energy and the Environment, 108 pp. $12.95
Habitats: Where the Wild Things Live, 48 pp. $9.95
The Kids' Environment Book: What's Awry and Why, 192 pp. $13.95

Ordering Information
Please check your local bookstore for our books, or call 1-800-888-7504 to order direct from us. All orders are shipped via UPS; see chart below to calculate your shipping charge to U.S. destinations. **No P.O. Boxes please; we must have a street address to ensure delivery.** If the book you request is not available, we will hold your check until we can ship it. Foreign orders will be shipped surface rate unless otherwise requested; please enclose $3.00 for the first item and $1.00 for each additional item.

For U.S. Orders Totaling	Add	For U.S. Orders Totaling	Add
Up to $15.00	$4.25	$45.01 to $75.00	$6.25
$15.01 to $45.00	$5.25	$75.01 or more	$7.25

Methods of Payment
Check, money order, American Express, MasterCard, or Visa. We cannot be responsible for cash sent through the mail. For credit card orders, include your card number, expiration date, and your signature, or call (800) 888-7504. American Express card orders can be shipped only to billing address of cardholder. Sorry, no C.O.D.'s. Residents of sunny New Mexico, add 6.125% tax to total.

Address all orders and inquiries to:
    John Muir Publications
    P.O. Box 613
    Santa Fe, NM 87504
    (505) 982-4078
    (800) 888-7504